KHANEMUISM

(KA-NEE-MOO-ISM)

Anthology of Poems, Speeches, and Lyrics

Robert L. Woods
'Khanemu'

authorHOUSE®

AuthorHouse™
1663 Liberty Drive
Bloomington, IN 47403
www.authorhouse.com
Phone: 1 (800) 839-8640

Published by AuthorHouse 01/20/2020

ISBN: 978-1-7283-4346-4 (sc)
ISBN: 978-1-7283-4345-7 (e)

Contents

The Esoteric Definition of the Three Symbols
(front cover)

(1) The eye represents intuitive knowledge of one's self; symbolizing consciousness and the awareness of the essence of one's self and its relation to the material and spiritual realities of being. One travels blindly if one does not see and comprehend the twofold realities of life in relation to self.

(2) The pyramid represents the dual nature of the self at the base with opposite sides, gradually transcending toward oneness at the crown. During our lives we struggle against our dual-natured tendencies (e.g., good/bad, love/hate, kindness/cruelty, knowledge/ignorance, self-control/lack of self-control).

(3) The ankh cross refers to life in the form of a human being.
  (a) the above portion (the shen ring) means eternity, feminine principal, womb, magnetically charged;
  (b) the cross: that which is temporal, time-space principal, phallic principal electrically charged;
  (c) the ankh middle portion (knot) holds the two principals together, eternal-temporal, immortal-mortal, spirit-body, creating the human body.

The meaning of Khanemu

Meaning of *khanemu* (pronounced ka-nee-moo), original spelling *khnemu*, is the aspect of god amun/amen, as the creator of men. He sits at the potter's wheel, fashioning the form of all things in creation. It also means to join, build, or unite.

Acknowledgements

To MY BELOVED mom, Bessie M. Cruse: thank you for loving me endlessly. Eternal peace be unto you.

To Mr. Wylie M. Woods: you passed on to me your greatest gift: your baritone voice. I love you, Dad!

My deepest appreciation to my sister, Brenda, and brother-in-law, Mr. Arvell Charles: come sunshine or storm, your love never wavered. I am so indebted to you.

To Mr. Jonathan C. Woods: may your entrepreneurial skills and musical talents take you to heights unknown. I love you, son.

To my cousins Regina and Ethel, and my dear Aunt Mavis: I'll never forget and will always cherish your needed love and support.

To Mr. Yves Howard, author of *The Universal Power and Greatness of Woman and Her Rulership* (Cary Press Books, 2018), your technical advice has been invaluable.

Dedication

THIS LITERARY PIECE is dedicated, in this land of freedom and opportunity ...

To those whose ancestors came to the native shores of America shackled in chains of brutal bondage, who are black and gifted by nature yet are maligned, marginalized, despised, hunted down, caricatured, and discriminated against because of the abundance of melanin in their skin.

To those who fight, despite the curtailing of civil liberties, constant undermining of constitutional civil rights, ongoing right-wing-inspired enactments of voter suppression, ever-grinding gears of gentrification, and urban displacement of communities of color. To those caught in the racist vice grip of the war on communities of color masquerading as a war on drugs, backed by the corporate prison industrial complex and their elected yes-men officials.

To those bullied, lied about, demonized, and mocked by a wannabe fascist, racist, xenophobic, misogynistic president paying homage to the very national anthem whose aim was to perpetuate their chattel enslavement and condemn their human quest for freedom.

And to a very special group of patriotic advocates—fiercely battling for sociopolitical, religious, and ethnic equality—still possessing the audacity to rise and thrive, because America void of diversity, without the representation of people of color, is America absent a soul.

To you I say: Khanemu.

Introduction

LET ME EXPLAIN my motivation behind writing this book. Around the fall of 2007, about eleven years prior to my introduction to creative writing, an interesting lady whom I will never forget (though whose name escapes me) solicited my services as a freelance photographer to take a series of photographs promoting her hypnotherapy website.

During our initial session, she complimented the forcefulness of my baritone voice but quickly followed up with some advice. "You have a nice voice, Mr. Woods, but learn how to write. For if you learn the art of writing, you can write your ticket to anywhere you want."

Based on that encounter, and others of a similar nature, I believe some people we encounter can speak to our lives, regarding our abilities, as well as on our actions and behaviors through an intuitive, analytical, or critical approach, either warning or encouraging us in ways that can crystalize into reality. I believe this woman's encouraging words accomplished exactly that. Until that photograph session with her, I had not written anything in a creative manner, certainly nothing expressing my thoughts and ideas in a detailed manner.

This book, consisting of eclectic works of poetry, lyrics, and speeches is what became my reality. *Khanemuism* is the result of a ten-year quest to relate to the world through my words as joy, pain, sorrow, intellectualism, or love. *Khanemuism* is my creative lens into many subjects, including longing for love, celebrating the closeness of family, castigating the vices of political corruption, exposing urban crime, condemning poverty and economic deprivation, celebrating the power of sex and romance, shedding light on various religious institutions, and achieving self-empowerment through inspirational speeches.

Every subject, issue, and vice in our society and the world at large is open to explore, to exploit, and to ponder upon in *Khanemuism*. Whether you agree or disagree, you will find lyrics referencing celebrities, political figures, criminals, religious figures, as well as ordinary people.

Khanemuism also deals with sensitive and controversial subjects such as police shootings of black men, sex scandals, wars and genocide, and racism and gang violence.

Not surprising, for instance, is the ever-occurring vice of racism in America. Many African Americans and a number of whites thought (mistakenly) that with the election of this nation's first black president, America was finally moving toward a post-racist society, only to be faced with the naked truth: a white backlash that quickly moved from implied to verbal to a full steam of locomotive momentum, as witnessed in scores of black men being gunned down by white police officers. This is still happening without any real adverse consequences, whether the offense was legal or criminal.

With the recent uptick of whites calling the police on black Americans for engaging in everyday activities—like barbequing in parks, relaxing into their own homes, shopping in stores, or selling bottled water. Consider, for instance, the young black woman from my native city of Oakland who was sadistically attacked, her throat slit from behind by a white, knife-wielding transient man on the MacArthur BART station platform, with law enforcement and the media reluctant to label it as racially motivated.

The October 2018 Smith College incident involved a black female student from Africa, who got a taste of racial profiling when a campus employee called the police on her. The employee's rationale? "She looked *out of place.*"

This is language symbolism, as author and professor Ibram X. Kendi points out in his brilliant book, "*Stamped from the Beginning: The Definitive*

History of Racist Ideas in America", where terms such as blackballed, black sheep, bio-underclass, and welfare queens suggest blacks are subhuman, inferior, and intellectually challenged. This is something our current president, particularly during his rallies and online Twitter "tweets," consistently pushes. For instance, his ongoing attacks on Congresswoman Maxine Waters refer to her as having a low IQ, and he refers to basketball star LeBron James as not being smart. He attacks African Americans on all professional levels.

These racialized references to the so-called inferior intelligence of African Americans follows a long line of racist thinking (void of any definitive proof), starting with Greek philosopher Aristotle, who stated, "Enslaved people were by nature incapable of reasoning and live a life of pure sensation." This highly venerated playwright regularly put forth racist ideas in his plays (e.g., inferior blackness versus superior whiteness" in *Tragedy of Othello*; the hypersexual Aaron in *Titus Andronicus);*

Founding Father Thomas Jefferson, in his racist book *Notes on the State of Virginia*, which was widely read and circulated in the political and academic arenas in both Europe and America, depicts blacks, both slaves and free, as lazy, lacking forethought, possessing a high threshold for pain, and having poor reasoning skills, along with a slew of other ridiculous claims.

It's not inconceivable that after being fed a constant racist ideological diet, century after century, you have whites feeling and voicing the racist idea that blacks are undeserving to move and exist in the same social sphere as their white counterparts, except for being confined in their segregated enclaves.

The all-too-familiar phrases and clichés, after these issues of race prejudice is "We need to have a serious discussion about race," coming from the lips of celebrities like Oprah, news correspondents, political and religious leaders, and a scant number of law-enforcement officials, However, never in attendance are the very ones perpetuating these racist outrages. These so-called open-talk forums about race, oftentimes get watered down to tired old suggestions of "we must try to understand each other's point of view"—sadly but predictively ending on that note, until the next video surfaces of an unarmed black man being targeted and gunned down by a gun-toting police officer.

Khanemuism is my attempt to creatively express, in poetic fashion, these social injustices with blunt precision (for instance, in my poem "The Police Are Gunning Us Down"). Our forty-fifth president adamantly refuses to speak out against racist violence and has implicitly endorsed it, through his silence. On the other hand, he attacks black professional athletes for exercising their right to protest (Colin Kaepernick) and then turns toward hate groups (Charlottesville Hate Rally) with high praise. These outrageous racist behaviors are called out in vivid detail. So relevant is the verse from rapper Common's single, Letter to the Free - "Will the US ever be us? Lord Willing".

The very disturbing incidents of killings, either singular or on a mass scale, have indelibly transfixed themselves into the very fabric of our American culture. As we progress well into the second decade of the millennium, it is descriptively laid out in my lyric, chapter 3:7 "Gun Violence". It very well seems there will be sequels to come.

Most certainly, it would be totally incorrect to cast *Khanemuism* as a book of political and social protest. Large parts treat the intimate nature of love as a very important component of life. "To Love, Then Lose", chapter 2:8, is a lament on the folly and mistake of treating the one you love as unimportant. Making her feel unappreciated, and then longing through grief for what was once yours, as she moves on from the relationship, is something I can personally attest to. These lyrics are a call to men to honor, love, and nurture the women or significant other in their lives.

"Love Letter", chapter 2:4, is about a woman who writes a letter to her potential mate, describing her qualities, wants, and expectations in the relationship. He then responds mutually, expressing his intimate intentions to love and romance her, be her safety and security. These lyrics are filled with erotic metaphors.

The poems "I Was, Now I Am" and "No More Pain" chapter 6:9 and 10, are admissions of my vices and mistakes, whether in relationships with girlfriends, my actions in society, and my personal struggles with failing to practice the virtues of integrity and self-control, ultimately ending with rising to the challenge of true responsibility as a man of humanity and community. A real wake-up call for anyone refusing to take responsibility for their shortcomings. The rhymes are strong and explicit and are meant to cause one to go inside oneself to improve one's attitude and actions.

Sometimes pain and heartaches are our greatest teachers; they just come, many times, at a tremendous cost to us and those we hold dear.

A favorite lyric of mine is "In the Woods". This literary piece was written at the request of a solid brotha nicknamed "Jazz," who plays a mean acoustic lead guitar. Although I'm not from the rural south, I was able to capture the spirit and culture of country life, along with rich descriptions of its pristine landscape, with its backwoods juke joints, moonshine-drinking hillbillies, and soul food cookouts and the constant threat of being displaced. For instance, the line "Developers, like vultures, using bulldozers to destroy our culture. Slow chokehold on how we roll" rhythmically describes the expansion of commercial development, displacing the land residents and sectioning them into crowded urban dwellings.

The most emotionally touching of all my literary pieces is the one in which I will recite for the rest of my life. This special one honors the passing of my beloved mother, Bessie M. Cruse (may God bless her as she rests in peace). This monumental piece is titled "Mom's Dance with Eternity", chapter 7:3. This poem, with its metaphysical poetry, style, and cosmic references was highly inspired by my favorite mystical poet Kahlil Gibran's poem "The Beauty of Death." My hope is that despite the passing of a beloved one being a dauntingly emotional challenge to family members, one can find a deeper understanding and some solace as they work through the grief stages of their loved one's passing.

Finally, I still marvel at my growth and maturity as a writer, especially when reading my speeches and orations. I started writing poems as a way to express my struggles and heartaches because of my past mistakes, as well as an attempt to express my thoughts and feelings in an intelligent and insightful manner. What followed not long after writing my simple poems, around 2010, I started composing spoken-word poems. By 2013 I joined Toastmasters International and presented an icebreaker speech, one in which you present a four-to-six-minute speech on your personal life, interests, and the like. With my short background with writing poems, the transition to writing speeches was instant and magical. Toastmasters International provided me with a platform to soar as a writer, poet, and orator.

There's no feeling like presenting a speech and captivating your audience using stories with emotional appeal, which we call passionate delivery. Presenting speeches and reciting spoken-word poetry is basically the same; they are both performances. I now possess an advanced communicator silver award (ACD), and I am very much looking forward to carrying my inspirational keynote message to millions.

My speech "Men Rising" is a challenge and encouragement to all men to rise up and fulfill their human potential, to uplift humanity through love of family, community, and positive examples in society. The speech "Awake the Communicator Within" is meant to encourage people to develop and harness the skill of public speaking. I understand the tremendous power that communication skills can have to influence and inspire your listeners, as well as opening doors to untold opportunities. This speech, I strongly feel, is appropriate for presenting in every location Toastmasters International meet.

All in all, *Khanemusim* is poetically blunt, socially entertaining, intelligent, grimy, audacious, philosophical, sensual, and spiritual. It will make you laugh, shock you, inspire you, and provoke thought while sometimes angering you, which adds to its appeal.

My hope is that this collection of poems, speeches, and lyrics contains something of value for everyone.

Chapter 1
The Power of Maxims

Silence the poet,
And the people will disperse.
Erase his words, and the people will perish.

-KHANEMU

Robert L. Woods 'Khanemu'

FRIENDS AND ENEMIES

A friend will strive
To fatten you
With the feast
Of favor;
But an enemy will
Degrade you with
The dagger of discrimination.

A friend is bona fide by
The beauty of benevolence;
An enemy horrifies with
The hooks of hatred

An enemy is misguided
by the madness of mockery;
A friend is revealed by
his record of respect.

Enemies are identified
By their impudent
Indifference:
But a friend is celebrated
For his charitable concern

A friend is appreciated
For the ability to admire:
But an enemy is engrossed
In the epidemic of envy

A friend is respected for
His rectitude for resolution:
But an enemy is a constant
Collision course of conflict

Khanemuism

A friend safeguards
The sanctity of sincerity:
But an enemy is dogmatic in
The determination to deceive

Robert L. Woods 'Khanemu'

TRUTH VS LIES

A person of loyalty is a level headed
Leader of liberty,
A prevaricator is a persistent
Producer of pain.

A slanderer spreads scandal
Soullessly,
A reliable person re-evaluates
relationships responsibly

A person of devotion
Detests a deviant demeanor,
But a deceiver is dedicated
To dishonoring diplomacy.

An honest man honors humility,
A man of fallacy fails
in the fondness for fairness.

A mendacious person magnifies
misunderstandings mockingly,
A genuine person guards'
gratitude gracefully.

A fabricator forever
Finds fantasy in falsehoods,
A pious person has a penchant
For preserving peace.

A sincere man sacrifices
Silliness for seriousness,
But a traducer's testimony
Will terminate the truth.

INTELLIGENCE VS IGNORANCE

A person of intelligence is impeccable
at improvising ideas,
However, a mindless person is malnourished in mental maneuvers.

A person of brilliance will build a brainstorming blueprint,
but a dumb person is discovered
by discourse.

A person of perception is passionate about practical persuasion,
but a person of stupidity is saturated with senseless simplicity.

An individual of cleverness has the capacity to carry the
conversation, However, an ignorant person is
intimidated by the influence of information.

A person of eloquence will examine everything with excellence,
but a nit wit will never network with his neighbor.

A person of wisdom will welcome a world of worthiness,
but a fool is fascinated with flippancy.

A person of literacy loves the lectures of learning; However,
a moron is miserably maladjusted mentally.

Robert L. Woods 'Khanemu'

CONSEQUENCES OF ANGER AND STRENGTH OF COMPOSURE

An angry person is an
ardent advocate of
Aggression,
But a peaceful person
pursues a path of
purpose.

A man of rage can
be the embodiment
of evil emotions,
But a calm person will canvas his composure carefully.

A peevish man is problematic
in perceptibility,
But a man of tranquility
is a textbook of tactful thinking.

A man of madness is a mechanism
of malicious misconduct,
But a person of collectedness
is a charming character of civility.

A man of wrath is a wanderer of wantonness,
But a man of harmony is a heap-full
Harvester of happiness.

An indignant man is impressed
With illogical impulses,
But a person of placidity is a
Proficient promoter of propriety.

WISE WORDS VS FOOLISH WORDS

Words of haughtiness
will harness an upheaval
of hypocrites,
But words of humility,
will harmonize the
heroes of humanity.

Hateful words will
honor the hellions
Of hollow-mindedness,
but words of love will
uplift the lost souls
Of liberty.

Words of complaints
will cause a cascade
of calamity,
But expressions
of thankfulness will
tenderize the thoughts
of thinkers.

Words of idleness will ignite the idiots of ignorance,
But words of substance will sophisticate the senses of the simple.

Words of doubt will
demolish the dreams
of the destitute,
But words of hope
will heap happiness
for the heedful.

Negative words will
cause a neighbor to

neglect networking,
But principled words
will produce
a personality of purpose.

Encouraging words will
Elevate everyone to
excellence,
While words of cruelty
will unlock the cells
of cut-throats.

Khanemuism

MAGNIFICENCE OF INSPRIRATION

It ignites courage,
Gives birth to creativity

It envisions the un-seeable
It's the catalyst of determination

It has the power of patience
It is alien to negativity

It seeks to unite and to enlighten
It knows no failure

Chapter 2

Eternal Quest For Love

Love, sex and commitment, three essential elements for a harmonious relationship, the under structures of a healthy family – like air, food and water, who can even imagine a world without it.

___KHANEMU

A QUEEN – LOST TO THE STREETS

This is about a young sista,
who made wrong choices,
and paid the penalty,
Her life seemed so promising,
but tragically ended,
This is how the story goes.

Her name was Desirae,
Beautifully gifted,
in every way.

Personality to please,
Body of curves,
Destined to succeed.

Once baptized,
in sacred pools,
Now fair game,
for pimp gorillas,
Dope feign flunky, ·
to cut-throats and fools.

While dad ponders the news,
his doves caught,
In a snare, her soul's
baring shame.

Before this twist of fate,
Flowing streams,
of dreams of going places.

Went from honor roll,
to drug totting,
thugs and ho strolls,

Can't fathom pain and pleasure,
tied together.

No longer cares,
about higher achievements,
her mind's detached,
got to go,
Dope man is hatching his batch,
Desirae sprung for the trap.

Went from promising queen
to crack feign,
Sistas grasp the meaning,
street life's demeaning.

Oh...the beauty of pursuing,
a noble course,
Friends didn't cleave to her,
now bereaving her,
No friends,
Born for adversity.

Dad preached,
on storming the rain,
but wrong choices,
and illicit crews,
will summon the blues.

Her world,
at her fingertips,
Her folks now scratching,
their heads,
as she flips the script.

Innocence on the chopping block,
exposed as a hoax,
Pleasant memories,

Khanemuism

dissolved to tall talks,
and dirty jocks.

Family dealt,
vicious blows,
from the reproach.

Right choices,
never to be ignored,
While hell mocks,
a woman scorned.

None compares,
to a mom's mourning.

A queen and crack,
can never co-exist,
Desirae's one of many,
failing to resist,
Street life's not worth the risk

Didn't get the chance,
to pass on her seed,
Couldn't get pass,
crack pipes,
ho strolls,
gremlins in weed.

Once dreaming of success and fame,
Now spitting up blood and phlegm,
while giving trim.

Tossed up in sexual trains,
heaps of pain,
Inflicted by the gang-bang,
Now Desirae's insane, this is crack's end game.

Robert L. Woods 'Khanemu'

Mom often cries,
for the better days,
when all young
Desirae wanted,
was to go outside and play.

But a lie,
often takes center stage,
and dreams become passed.

Moms tears now,
burdens the soil,
of fallen Desirae's grave, this queen has passed away.

Khanemuism

NAKED FEMININITY

Your beauty,
in nudity.
Plush,
with ravishing contours.

Your neck,
a delicate column.
A stalk of cinnamon,
Mouth-watering.

Nude,
your shoulders,
A sleek escarpment,
A velvet textured rose.

Naked,
your firm twin breasts,
resemble stanchions,
posing erect.
Crowned with,
sweet raisin clusters.

Unclothed,
your stomach.
A layered silk bed,
a pleasurable rest.

Your hips,
the base of fertility.
Perfected and carved,
for sensual attraction.

Robert L. Woods 'Khanemu'

In nudity,
your bush laden.
Pleasure garden,
Seduces manly erections.

Lovely are your naked toes,
resembling carat gems.
Outlandish flesh stubbed jewels.

APOLOGY TO MY BLACK WOMAN

God created our physical world, making it breathtakingly
appealing to the human eye. However, He masterfully
crafted one of his creations in the makings of you.

It perplexes me for my lack of appreciation of your substance, causing a
rift between us. Casting doubt as to my true intentions in loving you.

Becoming so immersed in your erotic energy, I lost
perspective of your unmistakable divine identity.

Surely our yesterdays are swept by the winds of time,
leaving me alone to ponder in retrospect, my inability
to grasp and cherish your womanly essence.

"Sorry", is an expression definitive of my failure and shortcomings, and
so I owe this reflection to you, hoping to provide you with closure.

I must release you so you can be free to love and be
loved for the, magnificent woman that you are.

Wishing for you a life filled with bliss and
blessings with love and romance.

It is my prayer that the next brotha recognizes and
celebrates you for all the beauty you command. Be
totally intrigued by your intellectual endowment.

Hoping that he retains insight in reverencing your spiritual intuition,
humble enough to adore the comfort of your compassionate embrace.

You, my sista, are nature's finest resource and a potent
sustainer of a man's pride in manhood.

A nurturer with your smile,

An enabler with your love!

A healer and captivator with your sensual
caress: This for sure, I can attest.

All this I sincerely express because it's me wishing you to
swell in a state of perpetual happiness, even without me.

With tear filled eyes and a heart bleeding with sorrow, I
must man up and celebrate you still, for wholesome and
genuine was the love you once rained upon me.

Knowing and confessing it was you who brought only your best,
but I failed the test in reciprocating the love you so deserved.

Please, my pretty black sista, don't harbor ill toward me,
but only think of me in terms of a brotha who you tried
sincerely to love: but I was not mature enough to appreciate
your love. So, you were destined to move on.

Success be ever with you lovely sista.
You've shown me a true reflection of myself.
Thank you so much for loving me.

LOVE LETTER

Special mail delivery,
perfume scented.
A man's incentive.

Opened the envelope. Love encoded notes,
romantic tropes,
better than the soaps.
Woman, you no joke.

It's what you wrote in particular.
Got down to business,
mentioned commitment.
Got my attention.

Described your dimensions,
a female's inclination,
vs a man's intentions.
The tension no one mentions.

You seem like a sweet thing.
Make a man feel king.

Tell you how I feel.
I'll ether your sun rise.
Actualize your dreams.
Take command of romance.
Cater to your needs.

I used to be a deserter,
causing tear jerkers.

I'll make you matter most.
Never postpone your moments.
Be the one to own it,
guide your omens.

Stronghold your secrets.
Protect your vulnerabilities.
Be your security.
Solve it all when you fall.
Your hurts, I'll dissolve.

I'll erase what upsets you,
be a prop for you.
I got your back, boo.

Amazing,
My dome you probe,
what it holds,
unfolds.
What can be told.

Darling come nigh,
There's a dream in mind.

A mission erotic,
Passion eventful.
Sensually flowing.
A love suspenseful.

Relax in soap studded tub,
Caress your ruby toe stubs.
Lovely back rub,
With hot kisses and hugs.

And while,
Snuggled up and love drugged.
We'll explore positions galore.

How about,
A well-spring of offspring,
Even a dream team.

Khanemuism

You're a love master,
A man-master.
Master of my subject matter.

Sharing what attracts you.
We talked about taboos,
Don't do's,
Boundaries and rules.

My baby boo,
It's not being cruel.
It's two in this loop,
You and me as a group.

You're a hot debate,
Subject to relate.
Full on my plate.

Makings of a love thesis,
I'm still gathering the pieces.

You and I basking in glory.
Here's the moral to this story.
For the presence of your essence,
womanly intuition,
I'll pay your tuition.
For love's fruition,
That's my mission.

Seeing between the lines,
a chime in my mind.
A love epistle,
with bells and whistles.

I'll wash you in hot water fissures,
skinny dip with you in Cancun,

Robert L. Woods 'Khanemu'

Drench in your monsoons,
just relax the rules.

A letter with sensual adornment, rising
in me what's dormant.
Luscious, lusty and I'm loving it.

My baby boo,
let's start a love coup.
Acted on stage,
screen plays and the sound booth.
Don't care what they do.

A letter fettered with all ingredients,
loving you is expedient.

All will agree,
you're a sweet melody.
Loves prodigy.
Fore-told in a monody

I'm sprung on your letter.
When reading your letter,
realizing,
It don't get much better.

LOVE AND BITTERNESS

Yesterday, you loved,
me so endlessly.
Clutching me, so
tenderly.

Overwhelming me,
with your sensual passion.
Love felt eternal.

Now we are estranged,
in our affection.
Like a broken water main,
causing love's pressure to plunge.

Or a puncture,
to love's aorta.
Flooding its lungs.

What became,
of the tender love of my youth?

I was your,
fruit of delight.
You orbited my sphere,
with such velocity.

We professed,
a love unperilled.
Embracing bare bodied,
proclaiming our love,
in a still pond.

Now our love has,
dissipated to a charade.

We battle,
like two unyielding,
dictators in conflict.

How does a love,
once so tangibly sweet,
loose it's sweetness.

What would it take, to
rekindle our love?

A LOVE TRIED AND TESTED

Love is not love, relenting to,
the slightest storm.
It only stood in fair weather.
Our love can stand the storm.

Love is not love,
when it is rough and dry.
Leaving both lovers,
thirsty for affection.
Our love is well nourished.

Love is not love, when
it lacks sincerity.
Making both lovers,
long for the heart-felt.
Our love is genuine.

Love is not love,
when it is filled,
with sadness.
Leaving both,
lovers in perpetual gloom.
Our love symbolizes,
Joy and fulfillment.

Love is not love,
when it lacks devotion. Causing both lovers,
to starve for attachment.
We have a strong bond.

Though the storms rise,
whether in rough times,

The test of sincerity,
Facing sadness and gloom.

You've demonstrated, a love strong and true.
You're my best investment.

A love tried and tested.

MY MELODY DESIRE

Is love made of gold
Dimensions of the
Finest folds
Clusters of you I hold

You're my paradise
Beyond realms of fore
My reasons reached for
Prayed for
Please give me some more

My sanctuary of saneness
Province of pleasure
You measured your love for me
You're my melody

If you weren't my melody
Then honey didn't come from bees
Breezes can't dance the leaves
No chance of reprieve

Songs flowing mighty streams
Preceding glows of spring
Never to lose
The gleaming of its meaning

Stemmed from finest of pedigrees
Your melody's here to stay
X entwined with Y
The reason why
Our love won't be denied

Sip this potion
Love me slow motion
While I sail your ocean

Everything's fine
Because in this
Moment of time you're mine

Expressing feelings
Not feeling departure
Seeing how precious you are
And a chance to love
Time to move smart

You captured me
My precious
Paragon of persuasion

I've transitioned
To a new mission
Because I've listened
You're the reason
For my submission

No hostility in me
You serenated me
Your love serums
Vaccinating me
There's fire in me called desire

TO LOVE, THEN LOSE

Sadness surrounds me
Because of arrogance
And pride
She took a ride

Opening my eyes
My love went amiss
Through my neglect
Now time to pay the piper

Didn't treat her
As queen
She suspended love
Issues my pink slip
I'm in a hard ship
If only showed diligence
There be no consequence

Didn't follow her recipe
Now she's releasing me
Far from a friend
Agony's closing in

Should've kept her
Close at heart
Cherished her thoughts
Kept love hot
As a spark

Now on the out
Without the clout
Feeling pain
Of loving then losing
Never amusing

Just a slew
Of bad news for my crew

Love once in my grasp
Man
Why didn't I try
Before the well
Ran dry

Wouldn't have
These emotions
If practiced devotions
I've caused this commotion

Why didn't I shower
Her like a flower
Stayed amazed with her aroma

A woman god sent
Now gone with the wind
My love was pretend

My heart's yearning
Burning from a sad lesson
The lesson of loving, then losing

Time to look inside
To see
What misguided me

Once loving me unconditionally
Now fleeing from me
I've caused this misery

Sporting shades
Disguising wounded eyes

Khanemuism

Reflecting mirrors of my soul
My pride came to a fold

Too foolish
To count the cost
Now all I have
Are memories of a love lost

Taking swigs of spirits
Is temporary appeasement
Without an achievement

Going crazy
She's roaming free
Without the love of me

Serenating sad melodies
Of a love blown
To the wind
Lost my best friend

Pain won't relent
Cause our love's past tense

Can't believe
This love
Went from warm and nice
Too cold as ice

Now paying the price
For my wandering vice,
Why did I roll this dice?

Don't know what to do
This ill will
Has blossomed full bloom

Robert L. Woods 'Khanemu'

My mind's in
Full fog
Total gloom
Devastated doom

My pains storms like rain
Veiled in darkness
My heart echoes with pain
Calling her name

DEFINITIONS OF YOU

My golden rose
Heaven knows
Can't believe my love you chose

Love phenomenon
No comparison

Can't battle your ecstasy
Never cliché
Love won't fade away

Your scent on my pillow
My treasured willow
More than a fling
Between us
Love's billowing

From the village
Of righteous mothers
Soulful brothers

Lady butterfly
Dancing across my morning sky

Friction in my soul
Love's taking toll
Stuck in a convicted role
Definitions of the essence of you

What is, is what it is
Grown from a child of destiny
To my sweetest reality

Robert L. Woods 'Khanemu'

Glad I was home
When you knocked
Thoughts of you, umm!
Sends aftershocks

Our destiny
On tabled discussions

Minds entwined
Bodies vibe
Loves sigh of relief

It's you I believe
And you believe in me

No illusions
Or confusions, just a
Balm ass love fusion

Blood of my blood
Flesh of my flesh
Bursting forth
From the bloom of the womb

Becoming the soul
Of my woman

Loving the essence of your soul
Visions of you
As my songbird
Heaven's bird

My sweet honeybird
Fly high, spread the word

Khanemuism

Our love's in flight
Realm's all night
Together awake
To an easy breeze
You're so dam good to me

Gazing on the morning rays
Perpetual lovers
Throughout our days

Yes, yes, dreaming
Of the definitions of you

Robert L. Woods 'Khanemu'

SHE CALLED ME DADDY

Made love to my boo
She called me daddy
Boo what are you saying?
looked in her face
She was not playing

Blowing my mind
Cause a dad's one of a kind

Babe
I love how you
Make my nature rise
Leave me mesmerized
I need you to confide
In me completely

That was all it took
My babe opened like a book

Told me the scoop
Daddy wasn't never around
My heart pounded
Shocked by the sound of it
Because my boo seemed well rounded

Told my baby
I feel what you're saying
Please don't misunderstand
But I'm not trying to be that man

With tears on her face
Said she misses him so much

Khanemuism

Lost in her search
Turned back from the pain of hurt
Though she lacked worth
Wanting to be his little girl

Now grown up
Her emotions woven in disappointment
Now I've been appointed

Holding her close
Easing her pain
Taking her high with desire
This woman lights my fire

Calling me daddy was joy and pain
Then she came
Now I'll never be the same

Since she suffered from
Fatherly abandonment
Showing her she's my heaven sent
And my love will never relent

If that's what it takes
Keep saying it baby
And I'll keep on bringing it baby

A crush to my girl's self-worth
When dad forsakes the home turf

So, I'm raising her up
Being her crutch
Loving her like my woman girl
My pearl precious

Daddy's home to rock your world

Robert L. Woods 'Khanemu'

LOVE OF MY YOUTH

Embracing palms caress
In states of velvet utopia
Our bodies swaying
In rhythmic patterns

Oh, how I searched you
Gestured for the love of you

Indelibly happy
Drenched in your pluvial rain
Immersed in your affection

Feeling your thoughts
Your desires
Empathizing with your fears
Love having you near

What a miracle
The workings of a love
So divine

Your eyes like shimmering jade
Summons me to your mystic embrace
I'm forever calm in your presence

DANCE WITH A DIVA

My black tie dangles
Barely clinging to my
Drenched shirt
Unbuttoned for a
Desperate relief of a
Still breeze

Can't fathom spending
My entire night
Embraced with
A lady of such allure

Man, what a lovely female
That apprehended my whole being

The two of us
Engaged in somatic flowing
Like two waterspouts entwined
Peacefully swaying

Oh, that dressed glistened so
To the night light twirling
My mind still dazed
By remembrance of
Such an astounding night

Violet painted lips impressed
On that sparkling glass
Leaves me smiling

Oh, what a breathtaking
Aroma scented in the air
For I've danced with a diva

Robert L. Woods 'Khanemu'

FLESH ON PARADE

Fragile spirits suffocating
In layers of carnal allure

Sensual magnetism prancing unparalleled
In selfish states of admiration
Tainted in envy

Swayed by affections
Of physical facades
When beauty fades
Remember my factuals at face value

Immersed evaluating physical perfection
Eluding emotional essence

Fashion Fare will fade
Along with deceptive charades
Please no more flesh on parade
What matters is the inner-grade

Moving me most
The soul essence of my peers
Loss of beauty
Shouldn't be the biggest of fears
Let this truth reign crystal clear

Seems every place you look
Flesh on parade
Is being displayed
Like an overflowing cascade

Gazing into the face
I cut through the chase
Longing to connect to the inner-base

Khanemuism

It's the inner beauty
I've learned to cherish
For the outer beauty
Will definitely perish

Robert L. Woods 'Khanemu'

PLEASE ACCEPT MY APOLOGY

Please accept my apology
Don't want to lose my family
Lost in my fantasies
Reality you gave back to me

I've made a mess
Lust infested
Your love I neglected

Boo
I'm feeling the blues
Fooled around
Played the clown
While my babe was down
I was running the town

You stormed my weather
Gave me your cream and cheddar
To hell with better

I'm writing anthologies
Filled with apologies
Painful transgressions

I've made the wrong impression
Intersession I need
I've learned my lesson

Am I losing you?
What was I thinking,
Leaving you all alone
To answer your moans?
Babe, I was wrong!

Khanemuism

Please accept my apology
And I'll restore what's missing.
I'm missing your kissing

As far as I can see
You never wronged me
Thought I wanted to be free
Until you contemplated leaving me

I'm seeing the illusion
That gave me confusion
I've reached the conclusion
I'm losing you

Faced with reality
Rethinking my priorities
Missing your sensitivity and honesty

I've caused all this pain and pressure
I'm trying to lesson it
By confessing

I'm restoring my credibility
By showing humility
Is there a possibility you'll stay with me?

Give us another try
And I'll put love in overdrive

See the world through your eyes
Chop your sorrows down to size

Hell no, boo
I don't want my cake
And eat it too
All I want is you
Please don't leave me boo

CIVILIZED BY LOVE

A savage,
I was before,
your love refined me.

Before your sweet,
serene love,
I wandered endlessly,
In states of bitterness.
Then you shed,
your comforting light on me.

Lost in a sea of,
companion killers.
Defiled by an orgy,
of pleasure mongers.

You showed,
me a better way.
A true pleasure,
of love and commitment.

My life was,
a travesty.
You rescued,
me from this tragedy.

Impeccable,
is your gentle embrace.
So delightful,
so wonderfully,
pure in sincerity.

Khanemuism

Energizing me,
I have eyes,
seeing how sweet,
love can be,

Civilized by your love.

Robert L. Woods 'Khanemu'

TOAST TO MY LOVER

Babe, come close
Lend me your ear
There's plenty to share,
Nothing to fear.

Urging me to share feelings,
Something hard to do
I'd rather hide,
Cower to my pride

Scared of commitment
Feared the intimate
Dreaded love's sentiments

Couldn't make sense of it
When love became intense
I called it quits

To me,
Love was an emotion
To reject.
Love was suspect
Deserved no respect
Silly me no empathy

Thinking
Real men don't fall in love
I was wrong
I've conquered my ego
Now my love has grown

Teaching me about closeness
About caring
Opening up is to man up

Khanemuism

Man's role is to be bold
Respect and protect her
Care from depths of his soul
Self-control under heavy loads

Putting her first
Satisfies your thirst
That's how it works

Love will never bust
When there's trust

My lovely guide
Beautiful sun rise
My woman God-sent

When it came to love
Having no clue
Then you came into my life

Three cheers for you
Who you are, what you've done,
Continue to do

Giving love in its purest form
Too deep to measure
Umm, what a treasured pleasure

A work in progress
You came with patience
Understanding
Working wonders

Not dismayed by my blundering ways
Seeing potential in me
All I could be

Robert L. Woods 'Khanemu'

It's simple and plain
When a woman complains
Something's strange
Her man's not the same

His love's gone from flame
To a smolder
Giving cold-shoulders
Feeling like a dead weight boulder

Soon love is lost
Ocean tossed
Like a lifeless rose
Washed ashore
A flower no more

True love's consistent
Filled with principles
No one's invincible

Love has dimensions
Destinations
More than the constellations
It takes patience

Understanding
Because some things not what they seem

Those in freakish fantasies
Lusting for a rush
Go from boom to bust

Enmeshed in a mess
Bogged in regret
Passion thrashed
Feelings trashed

Khanemuism

You're my savior
Love navigator
Not more girl chaser
my playing days on waiver

who me a pretender?
I surrender

You pealed back my layers
Deep in a sub-conscious sleep
Blessings to you
My lady of truth

Here's to you
Delicious shake and bake
My sweet Duncan Hines cake
No need to escape
I'm safe in your embrace

I told my mother
There's no other

Having someone to boast of
Long for
For the love of you

Chapter 3

The Socio-Political Realm (Urban Elements)

"Freedom without boundaries is actually prison without cells."

— KHAMEMU

THE PURGE

Dogmas, Drama
no love for scripture
peace the last we seek

Bustas who fleece
victim to shooter
too many Freddie Kruger's
Many Jews popped by the
German Luger.

Kids popping kids
Kids popping Ritalin
rise of the villains
School to prison pipelines
destroying our children.

Bring back common-sense laws
Economic flaws steep
blame the rich sons of Wichita
Unamerican Libertarians take all.

Muslim crisis
vices of Sunnite Isis
Radical feigns
extreme means

Shi'ites back to back
fearing for Iraq
Vicious throwback
from America's racist attack

Knowledge seekers
far in between
Tweekers feigning
Suckas trying to be seen.

Robert L. Woods 'Khanemu'

I'm the new arrival
fool, you missed my recital
Here's a thrust to your vitals.

Adore beauty
wallow in the gutter
with the color of paint
I'm Devil and Saint.

Poet speaker
knowledge seeker
with motives ulterior.

News going Celebrity
selfies with the wealthy
measuring our worth
by size of the purse.

Milestones of a tweet
dumb ass trend of the Week
Media creeps are rising
real News denied.

Bold predicter
cold composite Mack and Minister.

White Supremacists
ratcheting up hate tactics
sending Democrats deadly packages.

America losing its Democracy
unraveled we're becoming
no birth pain Nation
these are the Hunger Games.

Khanemuism

Vile hate denialism
the President claiming
White Nationalism.

Poverty extreme
vicious Gangs
fleeing immigrants
caravans ten thousand strong.

Wrong is Brian Kemp
Georgia black voters purged
Jim Crow resurgence

Ms. Abrams striking blows
going Toe to Toe
freedom radical.

Ms. Kelly lost her wits
a definitive
talk show host insensitive
Defending Black face
in America race hate everyplace.

My words are devices
like Cambyses
I bring the vices
Boss Swagger like Mick Jagger.

True to my flow
what you mean you didn't know
Better ask my folks.

Didn't keep society's demands
now blood is on my hands
Now I feel worth it
so I re-approach it.

Robert L. Woods 'Khanemu'

We're living in high tech
social cause and affect
no love afforded
fools and rejects

Presidents, Producers, Preachers
men of all industries
guilty of indecency
showing their wee wees
snatch grabbing
a male perverted society.

Now it's Bill Cosby
America's Dad has fallen
the movement "Me too"
is hard balling.

Mr. Huxtable is now a criminal
Judge gave him 3 to 10
in the State pen
self-inflicted womb
doomed he is.

There's another theory
it was a conspiracy
Bill pissed someone
off in the industry.

Peace becomes weak
hard to seek
when Murder spews it's heat

His name is Northfleet
from Boston's "H" Street
Gang-Banger turned peacemaker
popped by the Grim Reaper
who couldn't stand peace.

Khanemuism

7 days shy of 21
now he is done
for a ill Nigga with a gun

Society's Pillars
society's killers
from Doctor to Lawyer
can't tell Chief of Police
from a common thief.

Monterey Deputy
is a lustful creep
caught out his briefs.

An inmate screwer
protecting and serving
Sperm donor.

His Ass terminated
now upset
what he expect?
the law to shield and protect.

No peace for informants
no applause for a fraud
cast them down to Apollyon.

My Oracles metaphorical
anything is debatable
please don't breach my circle
I'm terrible
when things become unbearable.

Hacker obliged F.B.I.
by switching sides
through coercion and bribes.

Robert L. Woods 'Khanemu'

A rent a Snitch
flipped the script
on his criminal click.

Israel's swollen ranks
on the West Bank
Palestinians pummeled by Tanks.

Peace against the Wall
up against the Ropes
never seen a Pope deliver Hope
Got to find another way to cope.

Only God knows how it goes
how it flows
how my life turned
oh so for the worst so

Popping Terrorists
far and wide is a Patriot's pride
nothing as nefarious
than a home-grown Terrorist.

For all those who heard
let peace emerge
you just heard last words from the purge.

REALITY STARS

People hating
on reality Stars
saying it's not reality
but reality fantasy.

Calling Kim K cheesy
then Momma June
must be Super sleazy.

All that obesity
Country Bumpkin Comedy
low class reality
makes me
light headed and wheezy.

She needs
more than a makeover
a tummy tuck
cause her Super gut
done rolled over.

Fat broad making some cash
still acting like
Trailer trash
I know it's brash
but I got to smash.

Can't get a real man
or Bank investor
she was messing
with a child molester.

All that low class
Comedy trash
no wonder it crashed.

Robert L. Woods 'Khanemu'

There's no honey in Boo Boo
those producers made a Boo Boo
the show reeks and smells like
Doo Doo
T.V. fans under the spell of Voo Doo.

But I heard
as of late
Momma June lost weight
I can't hate
I think it's great.

Now hold on
Momma June is back
got busted with booze and crack.

MUSIC IN MY HEAD

Music astounds me
hear it all around me.

Music astounds me
I can hear the beat pounding.

Rhymes rocked my crib
toddler crazy
slobbering on my bib.

Music slang-banged
at my arrival
Rhyming is my idol
succumbing at my recital
are my rivals.

Nature woke me
with its bomb ass knock
Soul, jazz, Hip hop
is how I rock.

These Musical keys
showering musical sprees
no satisfaction
until Music gushes from me.

see how I prepare
mass producing my Melody
from Metaphors to Allegories
mandatory is my Music.

Drenched in the dew of it
quivering from the thirst
of it

every morning
giving homage to it.

It's past the passive stage
it's my pathological rage.

When spitting
lyrics on the Mic
Freaks go wacko attack mode
when my Voice climaxes
the main attraction
is my Rhymes.

Real hot up in this joint
so much groove in this
the focal point is my Music.

Music astounds me
hear it all around me
music astounds me
mounting with its heat
it's Music I speak.

Musical sounds woven
stamped on my cranial
can't shake this heat.

When my music peaks
I got to speak
can't keep it discreet.

Absorbed in its solemn prevail
more sacred than the Holy Grail.

Khanemuism

Awaken to Musical fevers
shakes and chills
a thrill for real.

I'm a Music breather
a Rhyme breeder
turning haters to believers.

Like a Star
dissolves into the Sun
these lyrics burning in me.

Churning in me
I'll never be free
nor want to be.

I'm stuck in its orbit
morbid it would be
if not absorbed in my
mental pores.

When music penetrates
my mental State
I'm not playing the Saint
hard in the paint I'm going.

Flowing so vivid
I'm livid
spitting so hard
Females tripping
cause they're feeling me.

Please don't rescue me
lyrics possessing me

my head is rigged with Rhymes
loving my predicament
Music is what I represent.

Repressing my Rhymes
reprehensible, detrimental
proud prisoner of Rhymes
delirious with my lyrics.

My heads in an uproar
crying out for more
hearing my lyrics will amaze you
inflicting haters with aphasia
can't mess with this
Rhyming major.

Expanded in multitude
Rhyming high altitude
Rhyming vast in velocity.

Haters have to go
hit them with Vertigo
My rhymes run this show.

Music in my head
always on the grind
never a day's rest
I'm guilty of this crime.

Eradicating ills
with Music's progression
using my lyrics
to teach life lessons.

Super sensitive to the Melody
Music dwells in me

Khanemuism

convulsing with spells
with this music.

Not scared of your
Smith and Wesson
or any choice of weapons
can't stop me
my Rhymes progressing.

Robert L. Woods 'Khanemu'

THE PARADOX

I'm dropping game
naming names
my aim is to unleash the pain.

Opening mad diaries
unlatched Pandora's box
the paradox this is.

No one is safe
from my vulgar intrusion
all included
no more ills and delusions

Hood morons and their peons
Car Jackas
House intruders
lifelong losers.

Going on the run
multiple baby Mommas
Bastardized sons
illegitimate birth ties.

The "Me Too" movement
is cresting strong
New days coming
The Boys will be Boys
club will be scrubbed.

Trial of Jody Arias was hilarious
a Media spectacle
justice debacle
heads shaking from L.A. to Morocco.

Khanemuism

Princess Di cared more
than being Royal and rich
campaigned for the poor and sick
the Royal click at odds.

The decision came
to throw her in the ditch
let it be known
the Queens a cold bitch.

I don't do fairy tales
so screw Goldie Lox
I'm spitting the paradox.

Tempers flared to a degree
between Solange and Jay Z
theories rise as her fists fly
delivered a slap
to the king of Rap.

Fake News Casters
watered down News
streaming lining
during prime time.

Treating us
Like deaf dumb and blind
those with intelligent minds
insulting them
Dropping dime Niggas.

A strange correlation
between America's racial crimes
and Nazi paradigms.

We're in a class War
race War
so I implore you to explore.

I'm much bigger than jack moves
pulling triggers
shoot up Niggas
become doped up Niggas
then role up Niggas
for crossing Niggas.

My Rapology is filled
with verve
make your vision swerve
affect your optic nerves.

Oklahoma execution botched
horrified watchers
the cruelty notch raised
taking pages
from brutal reign of ED Kotch.

Sterling was talking absentia
must have dementia
talking way off the cusp.

Said one we can take home
"Blacks don't care for their own"
we don't need a retraction
that's a call to action.

They can't stand
my verses political
Kiss ass comical
they want it.

Khanemuism

I'm bringing it
real ass critical
bad ass unbelievable
sucka ass unretrievable.

U.S. steep in discussions
shitted on deep
by the Russians
conflicted on issues
taking miscues
from Kremlin news.

The Masses
need cease being naive
like Adam beguiled by Eve
you're being debriefed
by my rebel stampede.

Putin's zero credibility
fueled by his cruelty
just like our police
going gung-ho
blasting friend and foe.

Oppression of the poor
Children orphaned
by the drug war.

Drug policies as social control
incarceration skyrockets
politicians filling their pockets.

When a Judge
lowers his gavel
a child's home becomes unraveled.

Robert L. Woods 'Khanemu'

Composing my notes to a theory
my thesis and delivery
harder than Steel.

A leader
rewriting procedures
giving head-aches to foes
dose them to a comatose.

No due process procedures
during search and seizure
police using violence at leisure
pushing us back
to times Nebuchadnezzar.

Remember when the shit drops
how I spit this paradox.

IT'S GOING DOWN

Some say I'm a lyrical menace
could it be
I bring major game.

Naming names
raising consciousness
to full-blown hypocrites
roaming realms of society
so I spit it with severity.

Court is adjourned
human rights overturned
shit ain't funny
it's all about Money
mass repression
Political hegemony.

I'm spitting lyrics veristic
synonym for raw rhymes realistic
you don't want to miss this.

My head is distressed
highly perturbed
my grin turned chagrin
won't be no resume
till freedom is exhumed.

Politicians of the worst sort
perpetual itch
like Genital warts.

Peep Senator Akin saying
"Most Women fake sexual assault"
euphemism for faulting their names

ricocheting the blame.
another Roy Moore at the fore.

Somebody slipped him a Mickie
he's talking dizzy
fizzy foam crazy.

Freedom is wacked
people around the globe
feeling the ills
injustice heaped
by tricksters in black robes.

It's not hard seeing
Who's serving this Chalice of malice
injecting the masses
with the illist of pains.

Better stand clear
the Vulture
is flying high with prying Eyes.

We're living in a social mirage
economic sabotage
dignitaries spewing
hodge-podges of stories
speaking rag-tag
fake ass Political drag.

I'm never afraid
to muddle the puddles
scrap and tussle.

They're straight out of pocket
wish they go out of business
let us choose
our course of redemption.

Khanemuism

The status quo stigmatizes
people in black listings
economic brackets
paint them with jackets

Letting them
advance to a marginal
economically barring them.

Psychologically scarring them
chances real slim for them
who's gonna speak for them.

Mocking their characters
with caricatures
it's long overdue
for a major breakthrough.

Employee goes on vacation
returns to a rude awakening
his job is replaced with automation.

These are common things
from tattoos to toe rings
from erotic taboos
hard core sex stores
excessive bling.

T.V sexualizes
they call it liberating
Moms exploiting their kids.

Chasing fame
monetary gain
not surprised
kids mentally maimed.

Robert L. Woods 'Khanemu'

Turn on the T.V.
not surprised by what I see
The President
acting insanely
claiming White supremacy.

Australian White Terrorist
slaughtered 50 you see
mobs burning our flag
with indignancy.

Film maker showed Islam a discourtesy
then ran for cover you see
scared of notoriety,
this the hate
the Western World perpetuates you see.

Still way too many people dying
come on people
open your hearts and minds
it's going down.

WORLD SCANDALS

Friends
Allies and enemies
open your eyes
to World scandals.

Corporate crooks in collusion
worse than thugs in Fallujah
peep game it behooves you.

U.S. perpetrates wars
against Arab Nations
all enemies
represent Black and Brown
started with the British Crown.

War on terror
is a code word
for War monger
often wondered.

Where is the
War on hunger
School closures
bull-dozing our kids futures.

Way past Iraq's invasion
the land is devastated
Bombs still blasting
out-cast Sunnis.

Infant mortality skyscrapers
U.S. leaves a hellish legacy
War profiteers
advance careers on Iraq's
pain, anguish and tears.

Who what and why
learn War Mongers secrets
until we die.

Too late
Arab Nations bent
on destroying the Jewish state.

Police warring on Communities
uniform insurgents
Vultures of the Shield
preying on Black culture.

Trump creating the perfect storm
Black Athletes attacked
demanding respect for a Flag
with that drag miss me.

Don't care
what the Princess wore
if she ever Whored ever
the Royals don't adore me
nor my peoples before me.

Three Red-necks
staring hard as they can
looking like Ku Klux and Klan
intimidated by a real Black man.

kill them slave Masters
scandalous and lazy
trying to enslave me
they'll be pushing up daisies.

F.D.A. pushes innovation
pushes back regulations

Khanemuism

people pressed to a consumer peril
placating ass to Corporate inventers
peep game from this lyrical dissenter

African women under siege
domestic genocide.

Violence soars
like running up score boards
horrid cycles
of Black Women death rituals.

Time to revolt like Maccabees
overthrow Machiavellians
cast spells like Macumba
poison them like a Black Mumba.

My lyrics never comes stagnate
flowing like Magma
mystical like magnifico
inform like Politico.

Pope quits the Vatican
shames the papacy
given dossiers on priests in panties.

Sex orgies
the cats out the bag
Priests in drag.

Strange episodes
of cloak and daggers
Church drenched in hypocrisy
cold cohesion of Popes
perverts and politics.

Two Popes
just bowed to the Black Madonna
America needs to abolish
this White Christ drama.

Human rights breach
economic fleece
in Cypress and Greece.

House Niggas
cheering two points in a Basket
in Caskets tons of Brothas
Blouse soaked tears
from our Mothers

I'm a Mystic
going verse to verse ballistic
given Black death statistics.

Digging deep
while society sleeps.

This is my radical appeal
knowledge seekers from the rear
World scandals revealed.

Khanemuism

GUN VIOLENCE

Colorado massacre happened again
looks like mass violence wins again
I contend...it will happen again
and again, but when?

Few days later
Anaheim police
put ridicule
and gun violence on a spiral
now it's gone viral.

Our violence is perpetual
astronomical
we need a revolution
fuck prosecutorial solutions.

Why is everybody silent
when Hollywood
glorifies gun violence.

An Oscar award
for brandishing guns and swords
no awards in a morgue
guns we can't afford.

Poor brotha sleeps in the cold
police become suspicious
riddle him with bullet holes.

Cold dead on a gurney
lost for eternity
cold blend of gun violence
mistaken identity.

Robert L. Woods 'Khanemu'

You'll know them by their fruit
lust for the shoot
sometimes
the color of their crew.

America is synonymous with
war and hate
breathing it
ingesting it
now we're sick with it.

Like fire
burning in a tree trunk hollow
hard cold fact
this phenomenon's hard to swallow.

Reason is out of season
treason is the reason.

Our national anthem now reads
we love greed

Home of the insanely seed
God bless
while we take from those in need.

Colorado theater
didn't have an inkling
didn't know his thinking
death comes in an eyes twinkling.

Gun violence is not on binge
this is the revenge
of the lunatic fringe
mass hysteria
a society coming unhinged.

Khanemuism

Bullets kill fast
Click, click
Pop, pop blast
peace is from the past.

Days of destruction
the new token spoken
shits no joke.

A radical wierdo
just smoked 50 gay folks
a club with no pulse
full of dead folks.

Bloody novels
captures our fantasies
loving the sequel
of its misery
violence is what we've come to be.

Bullets breach
pools of blood
tears foaming like soap suds.

Politicians lip service
won't give blame its name
I'm a lyrical flame-thrower
bad ass whistle-blower.

Screw Zimmerman's fake apology
should have expressed
this before the eulogy
Too busy concocting his story.

Gun violence is a chain reaction
worse than fatal attraction.

Sandy Hook
is in tragedy's book
bullets killed 20 kids
and the Principal
now peace is the criminal
my rhymes chime with subliminals.

Dorner popped two cops
and a couple
police bewail in gloom
burns his cabin to rubble
sealing his doom.

Body bags on back-log
guns supplying the demand.

America is rife with anthologies
depicting victimologies
political ploys
fronting peace as a decoy.

Two more episodes
58 slayed at Mandalay bay
32 floors above
bullets rained.

Blood splattered
scattered limbs
frantic music lovers push and shove
where's the God above.

Gun violence in every day news
killer popped 26
between church pews
Texas style.

Khanemuism

Quite typical
more in conditions critical.

Congress grid-locked
packed with side-bustering
political hustlers filibustering.

Check out my eulogy
my country tiss of thee
sweet land of hot lead
and killing sprees.

Robert L. Woods 'Khanemu'

THE WOODS

By my favorite water brook
waking to a Rooster's crow
where tall trees grow.

Soul food slamming
juke joints bump and grind.

Love my catfish
spare ribs
nothing like my country crib.

In the Woods
where family was raised
Magnolias provide shade
relax among the grassy blades.

Barn dances
where southern bells prance
Mom cooking it up
delicious ham and eggs
buttered biscuits
I'm missing this.

The Woods is high stakes
no landfill
rich country soil
fossil fuels
oil saturated
I'm so infatuated.

Wild adventures
howling wolves
crickets creek

Khanemuism

floors crack while creeping
poppa cussing for lack of sleep.

Nostalgic memories
family barbecues
dominoes slamming.

Kids compete in races
no sad faces
smiling faces
makes me want to trade places.

Cousins beefing over beer kegs
these memories leave one to beg.

Girl crazy
sucker for the nookie
ditching school
playing hookie
young sprung rookie in love.

Uncle Roy
strong as a back-hoe
master chewing Tobacco
neighbors more than a stone throw.

Sweet water wells
short trip to out-house
lye soap for shirts and blouses.

Memories run deep
nature's beck and call
dam...we had it all.

Robert L. Woods 'Khanemu'

Smell of Momma's cornbread
all her kids well fed
religious born...raised and well-read.

Country life so simple
work so hard
time off for choir rehearsal.

Sunday sermons
come Monday
Preacher drunk on bourbon
pulled over for swerving
which God is he serving?

The Woods
pristine and plentiful
Black Berry deep
Molasses' seeped trees
sweet honey bees.

Folk songs
harmonicas
groove to the blues
hung over from booze.

Mug bug muckin
pig feet sucking
wild boars roam
possibilities roaming free.

Fog casts it's misty gloom
the prettiest flowers bloom.

Country skies beautiful
then comes thunder and lightening

Khanemuism

so frightening but exciting
crazy storms the norm
since I was born.

Country babes skiny dipping
hillbillies creeping and peeping
dizzy on snuff
guzzling that moonshine stuff.

The Woods is wild and rough
you better be tough
or it will call your bluff.

In the Woods
snakes slither
winters cold bitter
I'm going dither
playing my zither
watching my dreams wither.

Developers-like vultures
using Bulldozers
destroying our culture
slow chokehold on how we roll.

Bare feet
dirty mud deep
grimy, slimy
who's creeping up behind me.

Straight danger zone
trying to save my home.

A country story
full of guts and glory

vivid descriptions
for my tomb's inscription
we've come to my benediction.

The Woods
where we live
with a country pride
or die trying.

The Woods is my home
this is where I belong.

Khanemuism

MY PHILOSOPHY
PART ONE

Ladies and gentlemen
scholars, criminals
this is my philosophy
truth be told
heads gonna roll.

I'm a lyrical time traveler
poetic unraveler
game enabler.

Church claims
to be the earth's salt
why the earths in a moral default.

Machiavellianism
terrorism
peace and safety.

Then destruction cometh
from domestic crops
to illicit chop shops.

European guns
steel and germs
too many pushing up daisies
am I hazy
or are the gods just plain crazy.

Constantly wrestling gloom
imprisoned in this fleshly tomb
thanks to the god of doom.

Robert L. Woods 'Khanemu'

Not rhyming to pump the crowd
but to lift the shroud.

Trump causing national scares
cuts to Social Security
Medicare
enriching his cronies.

A bunch of G.O.P. phonies
seniors and the poor facing a rout
Trump is selling them out.

Bring back decent labor
living wages
stop baptizing the prison nation.

Democracy is good and tardy
time for a progressive party.

Reagan declared drugs
an epidemic
that his ass invented.

Drug laws
crushed Blacks in its jaws
now Whites facing the same plight
since meth
opioids reached new heights.

They want enemies
now it's you and me
all one and the same
we're pawns in this game.

A twig and a flower
can't co-habitat

Khanemuism

like a gamer
and a fool can't relate.

Parents schooling their kids
at home
schools are killing zones.

My hearers love how I spit
gangster twist
philosophical mix.

False test scores
a blight on kids' education
what's happened to our nation
no child left behind
robbing us blind
another Bush domestic crime.

My lyrics packs info
like a C.D. rom
deadlier than a cluster bomb.

North Korea's
Kim Jong is young and dumb
fucking with the U.S.
gonna get his head wrung.

America only understands
bombs, guns
prisons and the flow of cash.

Imperialists unleashes
two weapons on the world's poor
religion and wars
raise your hands in worship
as we usurp your land.

Robert L. Woods 'Khanemu'

Six words for Margaret Thatcher
Ding-dong
the bitch is gone
end of a real deal
sinister prime minister.

Inner city kids
bombarded with fast foods
burgers and bullets
prostitution rings.

Gangster bling
chaos and crime
their psychological paradigm.

L.L. comparing confederate flag
to do-rags
the pants sag
faced a back-lash
for his sucka
ass lyrical drag.

Black women forced
into C sections
minority birth crisis
racial vices of Doctors.

Not about complications
more like the residue
from slavery's stain.

Endangering Black lives
better hire a midwife.

Society at odds
with conventional wisdom

Khanemuism

like an influx
of white kids with autism.

Amazing how life
keeps bringing its karma
like nature producing its larva.

My rhyming dogmas sometimes mystical
sometimes literal
mostly political.

Beasts of the Southern Wilds
bunch of country fools
with nothing to lose
feasting on crab and booze.

Don't mind the lady
but fuck antebellums era
carried the germs
of slavery's atrocity
no apology...my philosophy.

Robert L. Woods 'Khanemu'

THE POLICE ARE GUNNING US DOWN

Are Black Men and Women
doing wrong things
or is there a genocide conspiracy?

Black children
athletes and soldiers
suspended at alarming rates.
Whites never suspended
at the same pace.

Racism is not hard to trace
it's been in our face
since we came to this place
enslaved by the White race.

Beatings, rapes
lynching's were common place
why do they hate our race?

Descending from Kings
and Queens
don't mean a thing.

Now we suffer from the police
like Jews suffered from the Nazis.

Black Fathers and Mothers
feeling the pain
our children are fair game.

Sad narratives replayed over
best believe
racism has shed cover.

Khanemuism

Feeling the heat
when we walk the streets
I refuse to be discreet
we need to live in peace
without fear of the police.

For the execution of her son
a Black Mom succumbs to anguish
in blood splattered pools
post mortem
he languishes

Michael Brown turned around
bullet grazed
dazed with his hands raised.

Racist cop unphased
killer crazed
with no delay blew him away.

Targeted for driving
walking
even standing while
being Black.

Black boy shot
eating a snickers bar
police shot him for fun
claimed he saw a gun
searched and found none.

Police feel
if I pull this trigger
my promotion bigger
so I'll figure to pop

this nigger
another notch on my Glock.

Like tic toc
White cops killing Blacks
around the clock.

One way to survive
this killer fest
wear a bullet proof vest
hope for the best.

Viewing Black men as thugs
dealers of drugs
draw down on them
pump them with slugs.

Black woman beat by White cop
who would not stop
Blasted her with fist-i-cups
put her in hand-cuffs
reminded me of days
when they said the jig is up.

Poor Woman beat till
her ass exposed for all to see
this ain't land of the free
at least for you and me.

Racist cops attack while you prostrate
vulnerable to their whims and fancies
execution of Oscar Grant proved that
shot in his back for being Black
this fact no denying.

Khanemuism

Blacks seen as irresponsible
irredeemable
disposable
police never held accountable.

Treating us like common enemies
perpetual foes
killing us is their side-show.

Now it's Stephen Clark
gunned down after dark
unarmed...
in his Grandmother's backyard.

DA refusing to charge
killer cops at large
send her bon voyage
on a barge
let her practice injustice
from afar as she starves.

Racism is outrageous
contagious
like that cracker Jefferson Davis
racist goon John Calhoun.

Remember...
they beat and kicked Rodney King
like a wild beast thing.

These are Demonic things
of Herculean proportions
suffered centuries
from murder, hate, rape
and extortions.

Robert L. Woods 'Khanemu'

It don't matter
if you're Black or Brown
in cities and towns
the police are gunning us down.

Khanemuism

CHICAGO IN BLOOD

City of Chicago
where lake Michigan runs
Black blood runneth over.

Booming city crowds
gutter bound
pop, pop
goes another round.

Windy city streets
killers creep
too dangerous to sleep.

Kids endangered species
can't walk the block
shell-shocked
by semi-automatics and Glocks
sold and bought bump-stocks
pumping bullets nonstop.

Poverty stricken
lack luster living conditions.

Dilapidated schools
50 school closures
bulldozed kids' futures.

No bright futures
school curriculum
of stitches
bullet wounds and sutures.

Conscious numb
opioids got Whites

begging for crumbs
living in filthy dung.

City of contrasts
contradictions
block busting realtors
mega church pastors.

Orchestras...Symphonies
STDs...emotional disease
sympathy's race based
gang crime infamy.

Elevated trains
concrete soaked
blood stains.

Elaborate Sky Scrapers
Movers and Shakers
underpaid Educators
overworked Undertakers
Juvenile capers 24/7.

Race polarization
gentrification
urban renewal
means Black removal.

Unethical tools
for those who rule.

City of Chicago
6 NBA titles
time is vital.

Khanemuism

Long gone glories past
walk on the South side
might be your last.

Windy city
seems so pretty
instant gratification
North Lawndale's deterioration.

Where they read your last rites
Gangs rite of passage.

City of Chicago
no colored signs
midnight race rides.

Just urban blight
red zoned lines
and White flight.
sirens all night.

Kids easy access to guns
incarcerated daughters and sons
in hood streets
dope sold by the ton
Trump vowing
a White Military response.

In Chicago
we need real Black leaders.

Not sucker shows
from buster hosts
like Maury
Jerry, Steve and Cheaters.

Robert L. Woods 'Khanemu'

Making our minds weaker
depicting us pedophile tweekers
low life niggas
showing ass crack
sucking crack pipes.

Father absentees
long rap sheets
pants saggers
killing for designer sneakers.

Black stars
no need for blind eyes
this is Black genocide
not society color blind.

Pretty breezy city
misty feelings
not easy with pity.

Gave birth to Kanye West
now he's
laying on Trump's chest
like Daddy knows best.

His high class
uppity Black ass
Trump couldn't care less.

Excuse me
a rap yuppie
freak nasty Kardashian want to be
and Trump's Black puppy.

Cook County
jail overcrowdings

horrified guard beatings
conditions deplorable.

Black bounties galore
what the fuck justice for
if our rights they ignore
my Rhymes evens the score.

From there
Black cadavers straight to the morgue.

Hideous history
Black siblings under siege
Black Mothers deep misery.

Big famous city
known for sports teams
executive suites
Black kids broken dreams.

Chicago's reputation adaptable
to a murder rate Capital
unflappable I'm spitting it.

City of Chicago
where lake Michigan runs
our Black blood runneth over.

Robert L. Woods 'Khanemu'

DÉJÀ VU

You've entered the drop zone
of my danger zone
tread around my verse Throne.

Better pissed off
than pissed on
head and shoulders square
this is truth and dare.

Truth beckons
for its day of reckoning.

You feel you're swayed
by what your see
behind the scenes
carries the meaning.

No longer the land
of Milk and Honey
corruption is the
proceed of greed.

Stock market pushing
the illusion of money
absent the work
clear definition
of crooks and jerks.

The Bird is trapped
not by the Wire
but by the Cage.

Deaf dumb and blind
don't be

Khanemuism

Drug use the same
across racial lines.

Why Blacks doing
most the time
somethings wrong with
this Melody
Oops...free speech is a felony.

I'm not coming unrealistic
just defining the characteristics
of revolving statistics.

My hand to the plow
one chosen from the many.

Breitbart, Fox News
is for Red-necks and fools
with no clue for truth.

A slew of racial bribes
race caste divides
this is past color blind
stand clear
all the devils are here.

So, give Brittany Cooper
center stage
with her Eloquent rage.

I'm bring it real hard
with my radical bars.

This system is sick and rigid
age of collateral tragedy

like what happened
at Ruby ridge.

Dam right I did it again
I'm trying to win
you suckas get lost
in the Wind.

My Lyrics mysterious
like Stone Henge
baffling those
too dense to comprehend.

As long as N.R.A.
holds sway
many will be slayed
buried in an early grave.

Never seen the day
when Fobs
Snobs and sleazy Slobs
unite like a lynch mob.

All systems go
Irons in the Fire
my Lyrics harder than Steel
because they're real.

You just witness
Déjà vu come unglued.

REVOLUTION

People listen up
I'm invoking a cold flow
with super bold political undertones.

There be no redemption
hell of convictions
in my jurisdiction
all dogs on till my benediction.

I'm roaming far and wide
like the flow of a tide
in this age of a great divide
extremists creeping
from day through midnight.

Revival of tribalism
them against us
self-erected jagged fences.

Ideologies veiled in a fog
Human rights buried
deep in a peat bog.

The system judging victims
as criminals
symptoms of a system gone cynical.

Sexism White women face
many play victim
Black women face racism sexism
two headed monster
of a White male system.

Robert L. Woods 'Khanemu'

Drunk Carolina White girl arrested
pleaded and protested
begged for no jail.

Evoked White privilege
claimed pretty and White
3.8 College bright
a liquor head
claiming thorough-bred status.

Probably said
she has a White supremacist vagina
and she ain't no aunt jemima.

Prepare protocols
for this rebel protester
true game projector
no matter the weather.

Screw their lectures
school course books
my genius comes from reflections
raw rhymes and hooks.

Screw your religious
dogmas and creeds
I'm checking your actions
and deeds
then I'll proceed to believe
best believe
too many out to deceive.

Racism showing its symptoms
like a killer amongst his victims.

Khanemuism

Florida stand your ground
means shoot a brotha down
reason why
Travon's not around
state hate sanctioned.

Phantom jurist said
"It's not about race"
lying to our face.

Evidence showed
Zimmerman persisted
bitch-you got it real twisted.

A national crisis
ordered hit
by the Saudi prince.

Like we were born last night
saying he died in a fist fight
murder conspiracy
on the life of Khashoggi.

Trump needs to admit a cover up
or shut the fuck up.

No passivity when facing calamity
it's audacity I'm pumping.

I memorize like Memorex
verbalize from midnight to sunrise
spitting the whole text.

Super-mergers
hostile takeovers
fucked over consumers

fewer choices
radical voices needed.

Entertainment TV
a subliminal enslavement
of your mind.

A device for mind control
producing human trolls
I give blows to the status quo.

These corporate leeches
clocking like tic toc
bleeding us for dollars
time for the Revolution to drop.

In the age of mass shootings
Santorum talking about C.P.R. classes
sounding like an ass.

All liberal hands on deck
clinched fist
political vigilance.

This is our last resort
racist packing the Supreme court.

I'm from Oakland
where the Raiders started
packed Warrior crowds
with baller all stars.

My back against the wall
feet firm to the ground
bracing in position
and my rebel mission.

Khanemuism

Real critical news
the Jesuits handed Hitler
the Jews
Southern trees bearing
strange fruit
tied by bloody nooses.

A massive storm
formed when I was born
it's pain and bliss
in how I spit
Proprio motu
is how I move.

Baptized a Minister
but couldn't deliver
until I shook
my sinister attitude
blistering up and down moods
now high altitude I'm rhyming.

I'm a political lyricist
radical linguist
Rapologist
spitting hordes of metaphors
scores of incredible parables.

From hell they came
like 60 grenades on a chain
using race libel
cracker tribalism.

Corporate dealers
causing ghetto breeders
jungle concrete
urban blight.

Vicious weeds
crack feigns by the teams
sporting rotten teeth
and funky feet.

Crime ridden
poverty stricken
sickened by police brutality quickening.

A literal visceral
third world on our soil.

These suckas hating on me
can't stand my Rap analysis
my rhymes give them paralysis.

It's revolutionaries I eulogize
opening up my people's eyes
to a rise beckoning them.

From Mandela to Malcolm X
Nate Turner to Nkrumah
to King's visionary dream.

Liberty actors
ignorance redactors
spitting with dignity, for infinity
that's why these enemies bugging me.

With all I've revealed
we're racing against the clock
this is where
my verses end
the Revolution begins.

Chapter 4
The Eloquent Speaker

The large audience sits eagerly waiting the appearance of the keynote speaker. The audience is as diverse as the conversations echoing throughout the auditorium. In an instant, the commingling voices, amicable debates, and laughter succumb to an aura of silence. The long-anticipated speaker now approaches the lectern. All eyes fasten on him.

The speaker stands in silence, displaying a gentle gaze of graciousness. He greets the onlookers with a sincere, "Welcome to all here tonight." He takes in a bit of the circulated air, and with a commanding voice, commences his keynote address.

"An amazing new era has begun ..."

___Khanemu

Falsehoods, Lies, and the Fall of Brian Williams

JAMES ALLEN ONCE wrote in his book *"MIND IS THE MASTER"*, it compels something godlike in a man, who, through unwavering courage, to cast off the vices of humanity; who has put his own life under the scope of scrutiny; upright in his heart, faithful to his responsibility that he can be a light unto himself, his family and to society".

We will only know peace and security by mastering principles.

To my fellow toastmasters, and to our guests: While this quote stands eloquent in truth, as a moral guide, it often becomes sidelined in the pursuit of our self-centered interests. Brian Williams, the highly venerated national and international news correspondent became the poster-boy in 2015 of a falsehood, becoming infamous for falsely reporting that in 2003 he, along with other crewmembers, came under fire when a rocket blasted a hole in their helicopter, forcing it to land in Iraq. He repeated this lie on David Letterman's late-night talk show. He was eventually forced to retract this lie when he was called out by former soldiers who had actually served in Iraq. Why did he feel the need to lie in the first place? He had everything—fame, money—he must have wanted something a little more, like being recognized as a heroic, courageous newsman who defied death while being under fire by the terrorist network Al-Qaeda.

In the end, he achieved neither, but he did manage to sacrifice two qualities that mattered most: influence and credibility.

But Brian Williams is not the only one to be implicated in a web of deceit and lies. There exists no field or profession where someone will not have a penchant to somehow slight the truth, and this includes us. I must now prove what I just stated—for if I state something without proof, this would make me seem weak and ineffective. With that, remember the televangelist Oral Roberts, who announced to the nation that God commanded he raise one million dollars, or God was going to kill him? Members and guests, this really sounds strange coming from such a loving God.

My mother, sister, and I were members of a Pentecostal church during my early teen years. Whenever a member left the church, the pastor warned the remaining members that God was going to curse the former member with some terminal sickness; his sick plan was to keep his current members in a state of perpetual fear and submission. He unwittingly made God out to be an extortionist.

The powerful and eloquent orator Frederick Douglass once wrote, "Truth can be careless and forgetful, but a lie cannot afford to be either."

Remember Anthony Weiner, the democratic politician from New York? His political star was rising, then something happens: he is exposed for taking bare-chested photos of himself and then sending them to a young college student, behind his wife's back ... then lied, claiming someone hacked his Twitter account.

Some lies make us laugh, others cause us to just shake our heads, and then there are lies that cause outrage, like the one where Missouri Senator Todd Akin claimed in 2012 that victims of "legitimate rape" very rarely get pregnant because their bodies prevent them from doing so.

Swiss philosopher Henri-Frédéric Amiel said, "Truth is not only violated by falsehoods; it may be equally outraged by silence."

There exists no public arena where truth and justice are violated with more impunity than in the realm of state and federal prosecutors. Hardly surprising, for the world's number-one incarcerator in the modern-day era. In fact, in 2014, there was a record 125 exonerations alone. This is unparalleled. What's wrong with our system of justice? The facts speak very clearly. The list of political corruption, prisoner neglect and abuse are endless. Take for instance, the disturbingly high prisoner deaths in the San Diego County Jail system.

Prison Legal News reported in it's November 2018 issue, between 2007 and 2012, sixty prisoners died while in custody in the San Diego County Jails.

Disappointingly, in what defies reason and logic, instead of promptly addressing the crisis, the county officials decided to go after the award-winning journalist, Ms. Kelly Davis. Ms. Davis conducted a thorough investigation and made her report.

This is sadly characteristic of a broken system refusing to reform its ways, preferring only to sweep its abusive practices under the rug.

In essence, a criminal justice system which systematically engages in retaliatory behavior against journalists, who rightfully and lawfully uncovers its abuses for the sake of fairness in reporting, is hardly operating in a democratic fashion. However, has resolved to operate in a rogue manner, contrary to the common laws of decency. In other words, these San Diego County Officials behave as though they have the right to continue prisoner neglect and abuse with impunity.

For their twisted and selfish career interests, it's perfectly okay for them to ruin your career, reputation, and even life just so they can claim a victory on a lie. How would she feel if her life hung in the balance because of a breach of justice?

Toastmaster and guests, if the binding quality of law is its reasonableness, then this twisted ideology does not even come up for air. If you will lie, then you will steal, and if you will steal, then you are capable of murder. It's all about the circumstances, revealing the true character. Like what White South Carolina police officer, Michael Slager did to unarmed Walter Scott in 2015, repeatedly shooting him in his back as he fled, murdering him (see https://www.nytimes.com/2015/04/08/us/south-carolina-officer-is-charged-with-murder-in-black-mans-death.html).

It doesn't matter if you are a Democrat, Republican, police officer, or civilian—if this is any indication of just how corrupt our system of justice is, then please excuse Brian Williams, grant Bernie Madoff clemency, and thoroughly review every inmate's case,—state and federal—and justly but compassionately reassess their current mind-set, so that many will be deemed worthy to reenter society sooner rather than later.

Embracing Mistakes and Setbacks

THERE ARE MANY stories about speakers losing their train of thought, succumbing to brain freeze, and experiencing tunnel vision and dryness of mouth, an overwhelming feeling of wanting to escape. Most of these heart-wrenching experiences were alien to me while giving speeches. That all changed on April 21, while attempting to deliver my seventh. Those dreaded feelings became my very own; that overwhelming feeling of fear was so intense that I'm sure that fear far outdistanced any I'd felt during my harrowing six-day trial.

Some of you even came up to me and asked, "What happened?" Well, I have my opinions, but what happened was bound to happen, and guess what? I'm glad it did. That mental turbulence shook me from my tree of complacency and cast me back into the soil of diligence and growth. I call it my reality check, an opportunity to turn a mistake into a stepping stone for success. You see, that speech was not about growth and improvement, it was about racking up more projects. I did not prepare thoroughly. I had a great speech, but I had a haughty attitude in delivering it … so I stumbled, and that hurt.

Nevertheless, the very thing that causes us to stumble and fail can be what's best for us—no pain, no gain. These very setbacks contain the insight to instruct. Failures and setbacks provide a strong dose of reality, which can lead to humility. I know I need more humility. Why? Because humility keeps me grounded and my worldview clear.

I vividly remember an ex-girlfriend saying to me, "Rob, you're too proud. You may have a lot going for you now, but something can happen to lay you low. Mark my words."

So, God does teach fools, it seems!

I can still hear her words: "One thing is very clear to me: learn to heed life's lessons."

Failures and setbacks are great opportunities to know who you are, how far you are from your mark, and how far you need to come or improve; they are life's great teachers. Having power to make or break you—how you deal with them determines the outcome.

Michael Jordan used the failure of being cut from his high school basketball team to propel him into the legend he is today. He did not throw in the towel; he became determined, and as a result, we all know his superstar history.

Bad choices and a prison sentence did not detour Don King from success and becoming a mega-boxing promoter. While other inmates immersed themselves in cards and dominoes, he did the opposite. He studied hard, had a vision and a plan; failure was his springboard to success. Having the right attitude equalizes extreme opposites. In other words, success is great if you don't let it swell you head; failure is not that bad if you don't let it sink you into despair. We must have the right attitude about success and failure. We can fail because of arrogance, overconfidence, and bad choices, and we can fail because of lack of effort and planning. Effort and thoroughness is the surest way to achievement and the lack thereof is to be destined for failure. We must put our best into every endeavor.

Life is a progression of peaks and valleys. When standing on your peak, you feel strong and confident. On the contrary, it's the dark, dreary valley that tests your will and resolve. You see the menacing challenges ahead, and you know it's time to put in work. Therefore, when you descend into you dark, dreary valley of despair, know that if you keep pressing, striving, pushing upward to your summit, the peak will be within sight, within reach.

While failures and setbacks are inevitable, perseverance is a game changer. Great leaders understand that perseverance will pay off in victory. Perseverance is the constant flow of water that wears away the hardest stone, the bending, bowing but never breaking to the fiercest storm—this is your fuel for the distance, energizing you to focus sharper, aim higher, and push harder. But most of all, my fellow toastmasters, please hear me well: never ever give up.

Prophets of War

THE WORLD HAS never seen the likes of an imperialist super-power like America; the United States is the greatest superpower in world history. She is of a magnitude, dimension, and preeminence never before seen on the world stage. Like no other nation, the United States has military stations spanning the globe. For countless Americans and foreigners, America has proven to be an economic bastion of opportunity, a haven of religious freedom, a safe place for freedom of speech and self-expression.

America has and continues to be a great nation of immigrants, whether seeking a better life for themselves and their families, or seeking refuge from war-torn countries and brutal regimes. For many years, no other nation has produced in such concentrated amounts—in intellectual capacities and physical endowments—as we Americans. Whether in science; the liberal arts; politics; medicine; our magnificent space program; our legislative and judicial branches of government; our super-talented sports stars; our prestigious universities and world-renown religious institutions; our public and private schools; our hyper-glamorous performing arts boasting mega stars in singing, acting, and dancing. America surpasses the world. Oh, and let's not forget about our ultra-celebrated media culture, where so many have been elevated to cult-like status. America is home to many tech giants and technological geniuses. No nation is more welcoming and rewarding to those possessing the talent and skills in these industries, fields, and professions.

In my sincere point of view—even in my current situation, despite some complaints and reservations—I am proud to be an American. For those who might have raised an eyebrow when I articulated the noun, "reservation", please hear me out, for I will approach the heart of this statement as I progress.

Soon after the ravages and untold deaths, followed by widespread misery and starvation around the world, from World War II, the United States and the Soviet Union emerged as the world's most powerful nations, with the United States playing a pivotal role during the final allied victory. The United States became what President Roosevelt described as "the arsenal of Democracy." For we equipped the Allies with all types of military equipment and weaponry. Although the war had devastating consequences for much of Europe and parts of Asia, America and Canada actually prospered because of the war, including many southern negroes who abandoned the Jim Crow south, heading north to work in war plants.

Because of the diabolical threat of Nazi Germany and her coaxes powers with Italy and Japan, World War II became necessary. After World War II, America, despite its innate racial prejudices and discriminatory practices, and its reluctance to improve upon and provide social programs for lower-class Americans, seemed to be moving in the right economic direction, especially during the late 1940s throughout the 1950s. Many working-class Americans were enjoying decent living wages and affordable housing. The nuclear family became the staple of American cultural values, and for the most part, cities and suburbs began to thrive. America was the model for industrialized nations and emerging democracies. "Made in America" was a strong slogan, and our sense of patriotic pride was high, at least on the surface.

Then, like a boiling cauldron, America's social, political, and military contents started to spill over. American negroes, suffering hard and long under the crushing weight of racial oppression, started to demand a seat at the table of equality. Sparked by a tired woman refusing to give up her seat on a bus, the Civil Rights era was born. America, both anxious and obnoxious about the spread and threat of Communism, and fresh off a bloody war with North Korea, plunged into a war with Vietnam. The Cuban Missile Crisis intensified with the failed Bay of Pigs invasion, an international embarrassment for America.

President Kennedy was assassinated by dark forces within our government, and the sixties became a hotbed of civil disobedience, racial conflict, and massive war protests fueled by the continued escalation in Vietnam by the industrial military complex. Riots, looting, and staggering property damage from fires and vandalism would plague our cities, mostly because of the indifference from a government unwilling to make any meaningful reforms.

We saw the rise of the feminist movement, demanding all levels of equality to that of men, and when things could not seem to get worse, two of America's prominent leaders, Dr. King and Robert Kennedy, were gunned down. America was deep in a political and social crisis, which would last throughout the early seventies, culminating with the Watergate scandal. Interestingly, the suffix *-gate* would come to describe all other scandals following Watergate. Faith in government leaders was at a very weak point.

This Abraham Lincoln quote is prophetic: "I see in the near future a crisis approaching that unnerves me, and causes me to tremble for the safety of my country, corporations have been enthroned, and an era of corruption in high places will follow and the money power will endeavor to prolong it's reign by working upon the prejudices of the people, until wealth is aggregated in a few hands and the Republic is destroyed."

In America, there has always existed a struggle between rich and poor, labor against management, capitalism against socialism. Strangely enough, for most of the twentieth century, America has been involved in military interventions and occupations and flat-out war, from both European wars to questionable military skirmishes in Central America, to the never-ending "war on terror" in the Middle East causing never-before-seen breakdowns of governments, leaving millions upon millions of civilians at the brutal mercy of radical insurgent groups, displacing millions more through starvation and torture.

Now, we have an American president, along with his administration, who are promoting what Dr. King termed as the giant triplets of corporatism, racism, and militarism. The Trump Administration, which has been racked with scandals since its inception, has embodied a Machiavellian ideology or worst—under the cloak of national security, Make America Great Again, and national defense, pushing racist immigration bans, economic assaults on the poor and working class—even declaring an assault on our fragile and critically endangered environment.

American allied bombings in Yemen and Afghanistan and a schizophrenic buildup of nuclear arms—which no one will win—while enriching his cronies at Lockheed Martin and other mega-rich military contractors, with his war hawk generals situated perfectly at the Pentagon, we are definitely looking at another war in the Middle East or Asia, which will kill thousands of civilian families.

This leads me to share a story about the extreme ravages of war. As a kid, I, like millions of other kids, played with toy soldiers, pretended to be soldiers ... we were entertained by *Hogan's Heroes, Gomer Pyle, USMC,* and *M.A.S.H.* These shows were comical in their depictions of military life, even in supposed prisoner of war camps. Nevertheless, around the impressionable age of n-ne, in 1970, my parents took me to see a movie. This movie would open my eyes—shattering my child-like fantasy of war, rudely reintroducing me to the true nature of war, its merciless slaughter and grotesqueness, a two-hour likely scenario of war in its ultimate horror, a despicable reality we constantly blind our minds and hearts to.

The 1971 movie was *Johnny Got His Gun,* and within this gruesome theater of war, a torso of an American soldier was found on the battlefield, in a bloodied uniform, blown off arms and legs, blind, deaf, unable to speak, heart still beating, brain still functioning, able to reflect on his past, ponder his present condition, wondering if he will be able to communicate with the outside world again. For poor Johnny, the fervor and pomp of freedom, democracy, and justice spoken by politicians who saluted him off to war are now seen as the purest of lies.

That eye-opening movie was based on the bestselling 1939 novel written by Dalton Trumbo, the same writer who was blacklisted by Hollywood in the 1950s.

The following story is about the ultimate hypocrisy and cowardice of those calling the shots in war. Not long after Desert Storm, war strategist General Norman Schwarzkopf rose to celebrity status. He authored a book on Desert Storm and was clearly a decorated general, riding the wave of stardom. General Schwarzkopf, then caught my attention.

I paid closer attention when a story aired about General Schwarzkopf presiding over a Desert Storm ceremony honoring veterans. A dedicated African American Desert Storm veteran stood in line to greet and receive an honor from the general as he made his way down the line.

When the general stood eye to eye with the vet and extended his hand, he leaned toward the general, hoping to have his ear. The soldier, looking noticeably weak, whispered, "Since coming back from the war, I've been real sick, General; I can barely function now."

Schwarzkopf replied, "What do you mean, son?"

"I have so much internal pain, I believe I contracted something. I was hoping you could shed some light on this."

Much to his shock and dismay, the decorated general moved past the ill soldier without a word.

Watching this story, I knew something was clearly wrong! War is often glamorized but seldom told in its totality. Constant echoes of support for our troops ring out at professional sports events, from our celebrity-filled news media, self-serving politicians, holier-than-thou ministries giving their god-speed blessing to war and slaughter under the guise of God Bless America and the disguise of patriotism.

We see marines in dapper dress uniforms, snow-white gloves, sparkling swords arched high in salute. We hear chants and slogans like "Be all you can be in the army," or "The few, the proud, the marines." We make heroes out of clay, lauding their gallant deeds, giving them colored ribbons for acts of violence they carried out or endured. They are our make-believe heaps of glory, of power, bravery, and our self-righteousness, our self-appointed mechanisms to democratize and police the world. Those vets who speak of unwavering patriotism and serving are highly visible and celebrated, venerated and cheered. We have erected memorials and shrines to the god of war. We love to talk about the daylight of a war victory. We hate to face the long hellish night of bodies blown to bits, of children burned beyond recognition in villages in Afghanistan by hellfire missiles, disrespectfully referring to them as casualties of war.

We celebrate the promoters of war but never the prophets of war and destruction. Why should we? Their message is too real, too stark! Like the prophets of scripture, they don't tell us what we want to hear; they strip away our lies and fantasies; they lay bare our selfishness and hypocrisy. So, we banish or murder them, like they murdered Dr. King for speaking truth about Vietnam. We love to see stories of military moms and dads, surprising their kids in school, but they never report when the horrible news of a father killed in battle reaches the children—the sobs, the depression, the continuous acting out in school.

Desert Storm was promoted to the American public as a war we could win quickly and be done with; here we are twenty-five years later and we are still there, killing.

The never-ending war in Afghanistan is another prime example. JFK once said, "Mankind must put an end to war or war will put an end to mankind." A prophet of war declared the choice today is no longer between violence and non-violence, it is either non-violence or nonexistence." The image of a little Syrian boy sitting in a chair, shell-shocked, smeared in dirt, soot, and building dust, spoke volumes about senseless war—but he too was soon forgotten (see https://www.nytimes.com/2016/08/31/insider/seeing-orange-what-caught-commenters-eyes-about-a-shell-shocked-syrian-boy-in-an-ambulance.html for the image).

Henry Kissinger called Daniel Ellsberg a very dangerous man for leaking the Pentagon Papers to the *New York Times*, exposing the lies and cover-ups by the Johnson Administration to escalate the war in Vietnam, which resulted in many more victims of war on both sides. It has been confirmed that just as many Vietnam Vets committed suicide as died in it.

Dear Honorable Johnny, in the movie *"Johnny Get Your Gun"* wanted to be a prophet of war. This is how his story concludes. When a distinguished visiting commission of military brass comes by to pin a medal on what's left of his body, he taps out a message, saying, "Take me into the workplaces, into the schools, show me to the children, to the college students; let them see what war is like. Take me wherever there are chambers of statesmen. I want to be there when they talk about honor, justice, and making the world safe for Democracy. Before they talk about the necessary casualties of war, let them take a hard look at me and see what the call of patriotism has brought me and thousands like me—millions like me are the true messengers of war. The ones everyone needs to hear."

The Admonishment

THERE IS A truth, which many of you can attest to, that through love and affection, our family home will sing sweet melodies of laughter and happiness. But as a sad consequence of cold abandonment and indifference, our home can descend into a cesspool of bitterness and blame. Still ... there are those who claim that to love is to risk sorrow, for love sometimes fades or is never returned.

So, what, may I ask, is life? Is it not a labor in vain? Are we really destined for an uncertain future? Are our ambitions truly in-line with what matters most in life or what brings us lasting happiness?

I watched a TV movie about a young woman who created, with relentless passion, a fashion empire. Only years later, nearing the end of her life, she exclaimed with utter sadness, "All these riches I have ... it does not mean much. With all my material possessions, I have failed in the thing that matters most: having a family of my own. It's not my mansion and other sprawling estates around the world that bring me joy. I'd do anything to transform my home from an ossuary of dry bones into an oasis of childlike wonder; accompanied by their unwavering devotion, my life was a mistake!"

Her name? Chanel, the late French fashion mogul.

For many of us, it seems as though life is constantly evolving without ever being; some of us constantly search without ever achieving self-fulfillment. Spiritual leader and Zen master Thich Nhat Hanh once wrote, "Life is available only in the present moment." How true! How many times have we held on to regrets because of a long-lost opportunity;

failed employment possibility; an ex-lover or spouse left behind because we foolishly thought the grass was greener elsewhere? As a result of our unbridled regrets, we are sometimes unable to transition into the present.

How sweet and sometimes sad it is how songs stir up dormant emotions, images, and nostalgic memories. Photos and videos provide powerful glimpses back through the mystic cords of time. In 2005, I attended a funeral of an ex-classmate and football teammate, and during the funeral someone attempted to play a video of my deceased friend. Unfortunately, the emotional current became too strong; his grieving mother could not bear to watch her son within the theater of his former life.

Minnie Ripperton sang the hit song "Back down Memory Lane," and then some time ago I heard Barbara Streisand sing, "Scattered pictures of the smiles we left behind" from "The Way We Were."

Many of you know that when someone's home is gutted by nature's vicious phenomenon, fire, it's not the flat-screen TVs or the nice furniture they distress over. It's those precious wedding photos and family pictures, never to be replaced. It's disconnecting from our past we grieve over; it's reconnecting to our past we long for. We no longer own our past, and our future is but an installment plan yet to materialize! We only have today. Our past, however troubling, however sweet, are steps leading to the portals of time and experience, containing in them vital lessons for our lives.

Miss Ella Wheeler Wilcox, in her poem "Resolve," got it right by writing,

"Have you missed in your aim? well, the mark is still shining;

Did you faint in the race? well, take breath for the next."

Dynamic words for our encouragement!

Our divine ability to reflect, cogitate, and meditate on our lives, to place past experiences in their proper perspective should empower us with wisdom—forging ahead in the right now. The challenge of living is to strive for a noble cause within ourselves, as well as the world abroad, for what good is a man unless he becomes enshrined in the temple of humanity, from its foundation to its peak?

One of the most striking paradoxes of truth is that we gain by giving up something, yet we are sure to lose by greedily grasping on to some habit, some vice, some negative thinking pattern. This same paradox is what perplexed fashion designer Chanel during her diminishing days.

When caught up in the past, we miss the marvelous now moments; we must concentrate more on learning from our past and less on yearning for the past. Our past is the marble; the now moments are the tool for refashioning our lives into the perfect symmetry of self-mastery.

I have an older sibling, well in her sixties, who is known to harbor resentments from her past, even as far back as her childhood. She complains of having nervous breakdowns; unwilling to leave her isolated island of self-pity, she's entangled in the bushes of blame, irritated by the toxic fumes of bitterness. Please, hear me well: wallowing in debilitating thoughts of what should have been, what once was, is emotional suicide.

To live and thrive in the never-ending now, no matter where we are in life, with a positive outlook, is to be on guard against the vice of selfishness. Some of life's most disturbing incidents happened because people can't let go of the past and are too mindlessly lax in the present.

In conclusion, no matter your past mistakes as a parent, spouse, or citizen, you can achieve now, you can create now, deed upon deed, precept upon precept; you can build you mind, you can rebuild your character. Your past is but withered embers ... ashes burned, never to return. You can build anew.

Thank you for lending me your ear.

The Storm of Trump

THERE IS A sobering quote from the infamous former senator Joseph McCarthy, notorious for his 1950s Communist witch hunts and Senate hearings. "It is dangerous for a national candidate to say things that people might remember."

Actor Robert De Niro immediately took to social media, calling then candidate Donald Trump despicable and a punk after hearing Trump's shocking comments about sexually assaulting women. You bet he remembered, and you can bet First Lady Michelle Obama remembered when she gave an emotionally charged speech denouncing Trump.

Meryl Streep, at the Golden Globe Awards in 2017, spoke candidly about the anger, shock, and disbelief she felt hearing candidate Trump mocking a physically handicapped reporter.

Let's really not forget those middle-school kids in Michigan chanting, "White power!" and "Build the wall!" They definitely heard and understood the underlining tone behind our next president's hateful rhetoric. Since Trump's election, the Southern Poverty Law Center has reported hate crimes directed at Latinos, blacks, and Muslims.

Given the magnitude of race scapegoating drenched in white supremist undertones from Mr. Trump, with his high-profile appointments of Steve Bannon, Jeff Sessions, and Michael Flynn, with their extreme views on race, politics, and religion, you should understand the fear, frustration, and anger expressed by minorities. After all, Trump bragged that he could do and say anything he wanted, including shoot someone on Fifth Avenue, and not lose a single voter.

Interestingly, Noam Chomsky, one of America's greatest intellectuals, like a true prophet warned some years back, due to the overwhelming outsourcing of jobs, massive plant closures, systematic looting of pensions, and declining living wages, if someone comes along who is both charismatic and brutally blunt, this country is in real deep trouble— because of the frustration, disillusionment without any coherent response from government.

How did you think white working Americans would respond? When this leader says, "I've got the answer to your problems," or "I know who the enemy is"? Back in the day it was the Jews. Here, it will be the illegal immigrants, Muslims ... and always the blacks. Whites will be told they are a persecuted minority; they will be told they have to take back their country and defend it. Military force will swell; people will be beaten up. This is now our reality, and Trump has come along to exploit this.

Now the blowback is looking something like this. In Jacksonville, Florida, high school students who were not even born during the segregated south were posting White Only signs on restrooms and water fountains. Steven Bannon, Trump's chief strategists, had a hate website celebrating the confederate flag, saying, "This flag represents our proud heritage— post it high!" Trump built his campaign promising to build a wall along the Mexican border, causing many Hispanics to fear a mass deportation— like during the 1950s when scores of Mexicans were rounded up in what was known then by the offensive term Operation Wetback. So, you can see this fear is real!

Trump is rattling the high cymbals of economic promise with a nationalistic and protectionist tone—vowing to bring back good paying jobs in steel, coal, and manufacturing in rebuilding our crumbling infrastructure. It sounds promising; however, if history is a reliable indicator, governments tend not always to solve problems, only rearrange them.

President Trump has declared a proliferation of nuclear arms; so is Russian thug dictator Putin ... this seems unsettling. There are enough nuclear weapons to destroy anything breathing anywhere on earth—not once but twenty times over.

Author Martin Amis issued this brilliant quote: "Weapons are like money; no one knows the meaning of enough." President Trump has vowed to Make America Great Again, with much cheering from his supporters but many others suspicious as to the meaning of this euphemism. Many are eagerly waiting; many are dreadfully anticipating. So, when was America great? How was she great? Moreover, what constitutes greatness?

The Declaration of Independence, one of the world's greatest document, declares "All men are created equal" ... "being endowed by their creator with certain inalienable rights". Sadly, and hypocritically, this document was not afforded to two distinct racial groups, Native Americans and Blacks. This was a great contradiction! A great document in ideology, but not great in its totality.

As great as Abraham Lincoln was, he did not start off great; trying circumstances and unrelenting pressure forced him into greatness by signing the Emancipation Proclamation.

How great would America be without Abolitionists? Without its union organizers fighting for decent working wages? How great would America be without its Civil Rights agitators or women's rights advocates? Without those courageous ones standing up against unjust wars, without those who challenged the entrenched myopic, sexist, bigoted mind-set of the status quo. How great would America be without freedom of speech, religion, and the press, which Mr. Trump is constantly trying to weaken.

America has the greatest military by land, air, and sea in the world, but for the past fifty-plus years it has engaged in very unpopular, costly, and largely unwinnable wars. We have been great in waging war, but not nearly as great in taking care of our wounded vets after serving in wars. America is the world's great incarcerator, yet she is not great in rehabilitating and giving second chances to those formerly imprisoned.

In my conclusion, in Trump's home state of New York, there are more than sixty thousand homeless people; more than twenty-four thousand children sleep in homeless shelters. President Trump has, in his administration, a roster of super-wealthy corporate elites. They have the money and control the political levers of economic policy. He and his administration clearly want to make America great again for them.

The Lesson of Tragedy

PAIN, SORROW, AND tragedy are the dark shadows of life. There is no heart that has not been trapped in the clutches of painful tragedy.

Disaster has robbed all of us of our sweet presence of peace, causing all to weep the blinding tears of unbearable anguish.

Please journey with me while I explore this force to be reckoned with.

It was the summer of 1987, and I bought my first new car, a 1987 Ford Mustang 5.0. You can bet I was ready to show it off. One night I swung by a relative's house and spotted my little cousin. His name was Little Turk, just fourteen years old.

We drove around and talked, and when I dropped him off, he said to me, "Hey, Cuz, come get me sometime and take me away from this hood."

I said, "I will," and drove off.

That was the last time I saw Little Turk. Six months later, a jealous ex of some girl he was visiting gunned him down. This tragedy taught me a hard lesson on putting family off.

Tragedy is life's unfortunate reality, ultimate crossroads; life's strong medicine. Tragedy connects us in ways we can never imagine. The nation watched in disbelief when JFK was assassinated in Dallas, dreams were crushed when a sniper assassinated Dr. King on that Memphis balcony, and somewhere during these tragic interchanges, our families exchanged grief and pain.

However, tragedy has also provided opportunity for millions of people and nations. It has been both the demon of disaster and seed of development in the world, causing people and governments to realize the necessity for change. The tragedy of Michael Brown (the eighteen-year-old black man who was fatally shot by a white police officer in Ferguson, Missouri) has sparked massive protests for such change. Author James Allen wrote in *Mind is the Master*, "Tragedy raises deep philosophical questions about morality, the meaning of our human existence, and the control we have over our fate."

Tragedy produces sorrow; sorrow purifies and deepens the soul, and the extremity of sorrow is the beginning of truth.

Fame and prosperity have always been sought after in American culture, with happiness often being associated with riches and fame. But contrary to what is depicted on TV and in society about fame and riches, they do not define happiness.

The tragic death of Michael Jackson and the shocking suicide of Robin Williams underscore the painful reality that, to us, these two stars sparkled and gleamed, but the tragic reality is their happiness was an illusionary dream.

Nevertheless, tragedy is both interesting and entertaining, after all. Where would the monumental scripts of Shakespeare's tragedies be without the perpetual thirst of his audiences, past and present?

Surely the annals of our lives contain a composite of triumph and tragedy, from the very tip of California to the Mexican border. We, at some point, caused tragic pain in the lives of many. Why? Because of our criminal behavior, we were fueled by anger, deceived by our own schemes; we became allies of selfishness and ignorance. It does not matter what you call yourself, who you identify with. The cause and effect are still the same.

Now we are all at a crossroads. Life's hard lessons have been placed at our feet. Tragedy can be our grim reaper or our emancipator. Our decisions are critical, so my question to you and this great but conflicted nation is, what has tragedy taught you about yourself? Better yet, what has tragedy revealed to you about your place and responsibility in this vast world?

Thank you, and God bless.

Protesters, Dissenters, and Radicals

As long as the world shall last there will be wrongs, and if no man objected and if no man rebelled, those wrongs would last forever.

—American Lawyer Clarence Darrow

PHILADELPHIA BECAME THE center for radical protest for the colonies of early America, rebelling against the taxes and trade policies of their parent land, the United Kingdom. Dubbed the City of Brotherly Love, Philadelphia is also the symbol of American protest.

The brutal Ludlow Massacre, where Italian, Greek, Polish, and Hungarian immigrant coal miners, living and working under the feudal hand of Colorado Coal, Fuel, and Iron, were murdered. It was company that controlled literally every aspect of these hardworking miners' lives, desperately trying to survive they decided to strike, protesting their dehumanizing working and living conditions. Tragically, it all ended with sixty-six men, women, and children murdered under torched tents and merciless machinegun fire by national guardsmen and state militiamen— compliments of Colorado Coal, Fuel, and Iron.

Their crime? Fighting for the right to live and work as decent human beings.

A slave kept running away from his "benevolent" God-fearing master. After the third failed attempt to gain his freedom, his master asked, "Why do you insist on being disobedient and running away? Have I not been good to you? Given you sufficient food to eat, with weekends off? Didn't I give you permission to visit your slave mother down on the next plantation? So why do you continue to act in defiance?"

The slave—unmoved by his master's self-described goodwill, answered, "Your so-called kindness is irrelevant. I speak as a man the same as you. I have the same feelings of joy and sadness as you. I am a man as you are. The only difference is my skin is black; I want freedom as you enjoy it."

The master, taken aback by his unlearned slave's eloquence in defense of his case and unable to rebut his claims, decided to bequeath to him his freedom.

Rebelling against authority is one of the purest forms of self-expression, the essence of moral courage, human dignity; you must place your feet firmly on the ground, you must have skin in the game.

The Founding Fathers wrote the Declaration of Independence, a dissenting document. They represented our first radical thinkers.

It was Patrick Henry who said, "Give me liberty or give me death." No one but a radical speaks like this.

Thomas Jefferson said, "Resistance to tyrants is obedience to God." A tacit reference to the rulers of the United Kingdom.

Rebellion is in our DNA, and America is a nation of protesters and dissenters.

It is of no surprise that many African slaves, of whom I am a proud descendent, embodied this same rebellious spirit.

Frederick Douglass once said, "He who would be free must first strike the blow." This is geared toward both the natural and spiritual realms.

The price of liberty is eternal vigilance. Protesters are our trumpets of consciousness. Time and time again, protesters and dissenters challenge the cult of material wealth and the deification of mainstream ideology.

Martin Luther tacked his ninety-five theses on the door of Wittenberg Church, which eventually led to his break with the Catholic Church, establishing the Protestant faith.

It was the protesters during the Vietnam War who jackhammered their chants of, "Hey, LBJ, how many kids did you kill today?" into LBJ's mind and conscience as he slumped in his chair in the Oval Office.

Like it or not, it is radicals and agitators who stoke the political and social flames of much-needed change. The shocking murders of four student demonstrators at Kent State by national guardsmen on May 4, 1970, forced Congress to remove US troops from Cambodia.

For a population of sheep will in time surely beget a government of wolves. Sadly, America nurtures a puzzling paradox. We have forgotten about our rebellious heritage—producing the seeds—giving birth to this great nation.

We often celebrate our radical independence while giving the thumbs down when others assert this same radical spirit. This is what happened in Cuba when the Fulgencio Batista regime was ousted. This is how we reacted when the Shah of Iran was banished.

Dr. King said it best: "Western nations that initiated so much of the revolutionary spirit of the modern world have now become the arch anti-revolutionaries."

Our history is littered with examples. In 2016, three women college basketball teams were fined by the NBA for wearing Black Lives Matter shirts during their pregame warmups—protesting the ongoing killings of unarmed black men by police—under the duplicitous reason of violating their dress code policy.

Workers in this country paid dearly for their rights to protest—suffering brutal beatings, expulsions from company housing and jobs, and even targeted assassinations of union leaders.

Striking sugar cane workers were gunned down in Thibodaux, Louisiana, in 1887. Steel workers were shot to death in 1892 in Homestead, Pennsylvania. Railroad workers were murdered in the nationwide Pullman strike of 1884.

Because of their brutal acts of violence against these hard workers, it raises the question—did the Rockefellers, the Mellons, and the Morgans care about these workers, or was profit their chief concern?

These are our unsung heroes, and freedom martyrs.

Muhammad Ali was stripped of his title and vilified in the media, as well as among whites and blacks for his rebellious stance against the Vietnam War—an undeclared war—where, according to statistical data from the World Encyclopedia, fifty-eight thousand American military personnel died, along with 1.2 million South and North Vietnamese and Vietcong lives lost, woman and children among them.

The government tried to make an example out of Ali for fear that others would resist in greater numbers. But the opposite happened. He actually fanned the flames of a nationwide resistance. Now he is gone and we love and admire him, in part, for his rebellious stance.

On June 20, 2016, the US High Court illegally disregarded the Fourth Amendment, voting five to three to expand police fascist powers to search and seize on mere suspicion alone. Your home, car, and body are now open to intrusion. It's time for the masses to trigger an avalanche of civil disobedience.

In conclusion, the powerful, most of the time, discredit dissent and protestors, but human history, as Eric Fromm wrote, "Always begins anew with disobedience. This disobedience is the first step toward freedom, it makes possible the recovery of reason."

A Pretext for Murder

HANDS UP! DON'T shoot! This was the gesture displayed by five St. Louis Rams players as they stood at the edge of their tunnel before trotting across the field on their way to a fifty-two to nothing thrashing of the Oakland Raiders on November 30, 2014. While the crowd cheered, the players showed their solidarity with the recent nationwide protest of Michael Brown's slaying at the hands of former Ferguson police officer Darren Wilson.

The St. Louis Police Officers Association became outraged, calling the gesture inflammatory, tasteless, and insulting, even demanding an apology from the Rams organization.

Let's open this can of worms.

What is interesting is the St. Louis Police Officers Association seemed to be implying that the gesture was directed at them. However, there exists no evidence that this was the case. So why did they become so outraged? Was this gesture a threat to any police officer's safety? Or their family? I think not.

Now, we all well know that law enforcement and the military receive the utmost respect and admiration from professional sports teams at every level, and this will never change. As a matter of fact, our entire American culture, in the media, entertainment, religious faiths, and other organizations praises the work of law enforcement. In fact, I wanted to be a police officer with the Oakland Police Department while in my twenties.

Besides, the police and military are as American as apple pie, more so than you and me in some instances, so my question again is, why the outrage? After all, raised hands means respect and surrender to those in lawful authority. Have you noticed that when there is a school shooting, all the students and teachers come out single file with hands raised? There is an explanation for this other than to show the officers they pose no existing threat. So again, why the outrage?

After all, the police deserve some level of respect for the dangerous job they do putting their lives on the line, keeping us safe from harm—sometimes!

Unfortunately, we must remember that any sign of aggression or resistance when dealing with the police can lead to a deadly encounter, especially if you are black. In fact, I was told by an Oakland police officer that when stopped, it's smart to keep your hands visible at all times and act in a nonaggressive manner. I asked why. "Because being that you are black, it might not go well for you—not to mention that a lot of police are looking for an excuse to exert deadly force." That was what I needed to hear to be safe.

If Eric Garner had just raised his hands when first approached by those NYPD officers for selling illegal cigarettes … just maybe, they wouldn't have put that killer chokehold on him.

What about Tamir Rice, that twelve-year-old kid in that Cleveland Park? Just maybe, if he had known he was about to encounter two trigger-happy police officers and he'd raised his hands as they drove up, just maybe he would have lived to enjoy Christmas with his family.

Just maybe, when Lavar Jones pulled in to that South Carolina gas station, if he would have told that cop who demanded to see his ID, "Officer, I would rather you get my ID while I stand here with my hands raised because I don't want to get shot," just maybe that cop wouldn't have shot him either.

Just maybe, when Philando Castile and his girlfriend were stopped in Minnesota, maybe that gung-ho cop would not have felt the urge to shoot him several times even though he informed the officer in a respectful manner that he was licensed to carry a gun … if he had simply raised his hands.

Nevertheless, what was really disturbing was that 2009 Fruitvale BART station execution of a totally defenseless man. The very same platform I'd stood on for many years while waiting for trains. Oscar Grant, lying face down, cuffed, posing no threat, but for some crazy reason which makes no sense to anyone, especially to a mother and father of any race watching, as their precious child is casually murdered by a person sworn to protect, never ever in a million year would that be right.

Those NFL players meant no harm or disrespect to any law enforcement with their pregame gesture; they were just exercising their right to free speech while calling much-needed attention to a very apparent problem of excessive and deadly force that is pervasive throughout the ranks of police personnel in this great nation. Specifically, calling attention to police who abuse their authority.

Our elected officials, along with law enforcement, would garner nationwide support from the masses if they would honestly and swiftly deal with any sworn officer who abuses his authority and violates the civil rights of its citizens. For injustice anywhere is a threat to justice everywhere.

It seems to be the actions of both the New York Police Benevolent Association and St. Louis Police Officers Association that they care much more about image than about accountability. Instead of passing condemnation and blame, the associations would do well to search their own hearts and find the true motives of all those within their ranks who might be on the verge of taking a life, specifically those using their badges for pernicious methods and a pretext for murder.

Hands up, don't shoot!

Chapter 5

For The Love Of Family

The thrust of creation, throb of imagination,
push of inspiration, The beauty of poetic
expression

_KHANEMU

Robert L. Woods 'Khanemu'

TO A SPECIAL SISTER

Amazing
so much love
between us.

Formed from
the Earth's crust
blessed with a Sister
I can trust.

Closeness
so precious and secure
with all the personality
traits procured.

Made in the image of a Mother
the softer side of a Brother.

Always inspired
by your grace and style
that extra mile
you're so willing to go.

Your spirit
soft as a Butterfly
yet...sturdy
as a well-built fortress.

Possessing the balance
of tranquility and integrity
a Brother can't deny.

A sister is a complex
blend of a friend
and kin.

Khanemuism

Bringing this
birthday wish to a close
you are my Sister
for evermore.

Robert L. Woods 'Khanemu'

MOTHER'S DAY IS EVERYDAY

Mom...
there is not a day
I don't think about you
when it comes to you
every day is special.

You nursed me
in your womb
rocked me in your arms
nothing compares
to your Motherly charm.

You witnessed
my growth and battles
rejoicing in my happiness
shedding tears
when I experience
my darkest days.

Loving me...
praying for me
when I went astray
this is why I say
Mother's Day is every day.

When many loathed
the thought of me
you stood by me.

When the World
forsake me
casting me aside
your love kept

marching beside me
a Mother's love can't be denied.

Losing many family members
you soldiered on
loving me without a whimper
far better...
than a Christmas December.

Because of all this I say
Mother's Day is every day.

Robert L. Woods 'Khanemu'

THE SOUL OF MY FATHER

Soul is essence
soul is presence
powerfully felt
you are what soul
has dealt.

Who understands
the soul essence
of a Father?

Only the one
in whom his blood reigns.

Descended from Black Kings
beautiful African Queens
from them
your soul commenced.

From your progeny
many soul
anthologies are told
I'm part of that fold.

I cherish
being the seed
of your soul masculinity
there is no mystery
your soul's etched in history.

My childhood
witnessed soulful melodies
you sprung in me.

Khanemuism

Initiating me
with soulologies
of Nikki Giovanni.

Carried away
on Super-soul serenades
of Donny Hathaway.

Shook me to my bones
with funk from
Sly and the family stone.

I succumbed
to states of bemoan
when my Father left home.

All these memories
seems so sweet
I keep them on repeat.

You've given each child
a unique identity
now your voice
reigns forever strong in me.

Reminding me of your soul presence
the soul of my Father

Robert L. Woods 'Khanemu'

FAMILY LOVE AND CHRISTMAS

What is the meaning
of Christmas...
without the love families share?

Without laughter
without tears
without hugs
from those you hold dear.

Coming together to give thanks
with a hearty meal
is not enough to satisfy
that loving feel
longing to be needed.

While gifts are lovely
and certainly kind
it's the compassion and love
the heart longs to find.

Christmas indeed
brings a season's chill
it's the family love and compassion
that brings that Christmas thrill.

LOVE IS CHERISHED MOST

Love is not cherished
while sky gliding
on the wings of wealth.

Rather...
in the paralyzing perils
of perpetual poverty.

Love is not cherished
when in the havens
of heartfelt happiness.

Rather...
in the sunken sea of sadness.

Love is not cherished
while in the handsome
harmony of health.

Rather...
in the segregated shadows of sickness.

Love is not cherished
while in the fascinating
family of friends.

Rather...
in the lowly
lagoons of loneliness.

Love is not cherished
when in the refuge
of righteous relatives.

Rather...
in the fierce fangs
of foreigners.

Love is not cherished
when engaged in the
fantastic festival of freedom.

Rather...
when bound by the
perverse pains of prison.

THE LOVE OF FAMILY

There would not be
a person like me
without the love of my family.

All that I have
grown to be
was nourished
from my family's tree.

All the wisdom
from my family's knowing
caused my character
to shine bright and glowing.

As a child
love and compassion
were always celebrated
now a grown man
love and compassion
will always be dedicated to.

Like the sky
you taught me
love has no limit.

Come grey days
or come days of blue
I know love and compassion
by the example of you.

I often ask
where would I be
without the love
and compassion of my family.

Robert L. Woods 'Khanemu'

MOM, MY GREATEST FRIEND

Through all episodes
of my life
Mom was there
to support me.

When my life
took turns for
the worst
Mom was there
to pick up the pieces.

A love bright
as the sun rise
compassion so
delicate and sweet
as a blossoming flower
a Mother's love
is as a strong Tower.

Through life's rough terrain
it's Mom's loving virtue
that keeps coming through.

My comfort, my Teacher, my best friend.

Chapter 6
Struggles And Triumphs

The only answer to critics and naysayers,
is to pursue your highest aspirations and
dreams, until they stand above all like
towering monuments.

___KHANEMU

Robert L. Woods 'Khanemu'

THE LESSON OF FAILURE

Failure is a word
few want to hear
many flat out fear
still others
strive to stay clear of.

It can carry
a devastating blow
giving you
the feeling
of being the lowest of low.

There are many lessons
failure can bring
with much understanding
to garner
providing you something
worthy to cling to.

Failure does not mean
life has run its course
just another opportunity
to apply another source
to your life's mission.

Failure is definitely
not the end
but a new beginning
if you would open
your eyes
Take your mantle of responsibility
and reclaim your prize.

THE FLOWER OF LIFE

The dawning forth
of the infant bud.

Soo tender
Soo young
Soo virtuously refined.

It's beauty
It's splendor
It's possibilities still bind.

It blooms
It blossoms
Sprouting
It's buds wholesome prime.

It's loveliness
unfathomable
immeasurable
unforgettable design.

Yet...
the magnificent flower
has but a time to endure.

Today...
it's allure
it's magnetism
its charm is precious and pure.

Tomorrow...
it goes weary as it weakens
it waivers
it withers for sure.

Robert L. Woods 'Khanemu'

As with the precious flowers
of the fields and meadows
the same with each
and every human fellow.

PEACE

A Butterfly caresses
the Lily pad
it's wings
gestering with gladness.

Behold a Toddler
nestling in a heavenly rest
clutching a toy loved the best.

Windmills motions
with rhythmic ease
Chimes sings as it tingles
through a charismatic breeze.

The Moon dances a pattern
across the Mountain peaks
the Sun transmits
it's light to Rivers and Creeks.

Men and Women unite
in a moment of silence
trying to figure out
how to quell the violence.

Robert L. Woods 'Khanemu'

HARD HEARTS

Hard hearts
can't see
hard hearts
aren't free.

Hard hearts
no reprieve
hard hearts
all about me.

Hard Hearts
no forgiveness
hard hearts
full of bitterness.

Hard hearts
indifferent to empathy
hard hearts
full of selfishness.

Hard hearts
can be cruel
hard hearts
a blight on society.

Hard hearts
possess no patience
hard hearts
racked with hatred.

Hard hearts
for all the wrong reasons
hard hearts
oblivious to the seasons.

Khanemuism

Hard hearts
become broken
hard hearts
are tough people tokens.
Hard hearts
won't last
hard hearts
die fast.

Soften your hearts
or a wholesome life
you will never achieve
your soul will depart
from this world
in a state utterly abandoned...
soften your hearts please.

Robert L. Woods 'Khanemu'

THE SIMPLE THINGS

Men reach for the unreachable
and grasp it
they pursue the unachievable
and succeed
think the unimaginable
and it becomes the norm.

Yet...
the simple things they ignore
seldom reach for...
strive for.

In our affluent society
the rich are favored
much more than the poor.

Opportunity...
is drying up in scores
we criminalize
the minority and poor.

Justice is often at the expense
of being too expensive
love has become a word
hollowed in meaning.

Giving is seen
as only getting in return.

We do amazing things
like traveling to mars
and the Moon
yet we continue turning
our World into an Earthen tomb.

Khanemuism

We worship Technology
praise artificial intelligence
yet we treat or fellow
human beings as irrelevant
this is our human predicament.

It's not the complex
things we must master
but the simple things
we must learn...
must never forget
and never forsake.

Justice and equality
for all are ethics
we must practice
along with a general human acceptance
empathy and compassion
are virtues to live for...strive for
yearn for...not class status
and riches galore.

It's the simple things
that contains the most rewards.

Robert L. Woods 'Khanemu'

FROM PRISON TO THE THRONE

Through some bitter woes
many blows I've tasted
deep in oppression
can't fathom the frailty
of confessing.

Pursuing truth at all cost
with no time for flossing
my spirit immersed in turmoil
can't believe this misty world.

Chariots of pleasant change
take me to greener pastures
my soul's in need of ransom
more handsome freedom looks.

Teach me
to have passion
for righteous ethics
not the ways of scoundrels.

Oozing memories
of my soulful yesterdays
now pain has overlaid
casting its veil of troubles.

Nostalgic recollections
of my past life
now the resident
of stress and strife.

Through narrow confines
a bleak of hope reaches me

Khanemuism

I fashion myself
in its philosophy
taking on its reality.

Visions of a spectacular
treasure unearthed
becoming well versed
in my vernacular
while extracting its contents.

From bleak to a flicker
from a flicker
to a flash.

Shackles of imprisonment
cast from my past
thank God tribulations
don't last.

Pluvial rains redeemed me
setting me free
feeling no longer
the scourge of scrutiny.

Savoring compassion
from the almighty
on his wonderous wings.

Helping me...
to steer clear
from the gallows of suffering.

Mastering the marathon
longing for the long haul
a spectacular crown awaits my grasp.

Robert L. Woods 'Khanemu'

My quest is to dwell
at the last supper.

Pleading my case
that no one suffer
yielding up spiritual concessions
for the world's castaways.

My soul passion
to be placed
among eternal peace keepers.

This Worldly kingdom
not my dream to possess
with my innermost
to achieve the eternal best.

SUNRISE OF HUMANITY

As the sun sets
culminating another
page in your life.

The night brings rest
and a time to reflect
to be thankful for tomorrow
with a chance to start anew.

Going forth
in the spirit of optimism
encouraging anyone
who might be feeling down.

bestowing forgiveness
to someone who has offended
or hurt you
even visiting the sick
and giving comfort
to the broken hearted.

By doing so
you become to sunrise
kindness is the ray
that shines
compassion is a jewel
of humanity.

Robert L. Woods 'Khanemu'

WHEN NATURE CALLS

The dawning sun seeks
to provide a clue
casting its light
upon the morning dew.

A cascade showers
from the jagged cliffs.

The crystal blue sky illuminates
with stripling appeal
spectacular appearance
of a visionary state surreal

Amazing how nature
provides its season's call
from Winter
spring
summer and fall.

So vital for man
to fight for the ozone's save
or multitudes
will be damned to an early grave.

Khanemuism

I WAS, NOW I AM

Welcomed by the rich
and powerful
associated with scoundrels
and drunkards.

Dated noble Women
but slept with prostitutes.

Gainfully employed
stealing like a common thief
brilliant thinker
conjuring up stupid things.

I'm a man of contradictions
personality perplexed
who knows what's next.

Many opportunities
but chose wrong and the worthless
stood bold as a Soldier
ran like a coward
loved symbolism
feared substance.

An heir of society
dealing in the senseless and frivolous
hanging out with cut-throats.

Loved fancy restaurants
gourmet meals
shrimp dipped in butter
then shaved and bathed in gutters.

Gestors...
no genuine actions

thought I was a plus
I'm a subtraction.

Claimed maturity
acted like a childlike rascal
Eddie Haskell three times worst.

Played with Walley and Beaver
hard on for misses Clever.

Son of a proud Mother
reason for her distress
was I a mess? umm!
I plead no contest.

Confessed lies at the alter
then lied all the way to Gibraltar
straight departure from good.

Fed my essence to the Vulture
of pride
plucked out eyes
wandering blind as society's blight.

A World traveler
life unraveling
taste for the fabulous
on missions scandalous
decisions reckless

Trouble on the horizon clueless
near panhandler status.

A non compos mentis
in desperate need of a panacea.

Khanemuism

Night time predator
seething in heat
now my soul bleeds
for failing to heed
oh please
don't let my seed follow my lead.

My wonderful memory
of my terrible history
makes me sad and misty.

Claimed to be a playa mack
ended up a J-cat
had a bed of roses
turned it to thorns and thistles.

I'm a man of contradictions
personality conflicted
don't know what to predict.

Went from a Town hero
to ultimate a villain
only cared for my feelings.

Potential for riches and fame
instead...
slowly went the way of Cain.

Now...
many grimace in disdain
hearing my name.

Reaping the bounty of my days
surely paying for my deeds
a spade makes a spade
my troubles...
crashing down like the World trade.

Saying these things not a crutch
I messed up so much
so I call it such
who am I
judging lowlifes and sluts
in a rut we're all in.

Clutching vices like a feign
a demoralized demeanor
character unseemly
what did it mean?
answer came in my dream.

Self-wounds inflicted
battled strife
now I want a good life.

No more wam bam thank you mams
my inner core
much more in store
my reward
everyday living for
being true to reform.

A man of reflections
deflecting no longer
much stronger
than throngs headed for wrong

Reclaimed my sanity
humanity's scepter accepted.

Pride...greedy gain
I was once appointed
now anointed for causes noble.

I was, now I am.

NO MORE PAIN

Tremendous pain
visiting my yesterdays
nevertheless
necessary for my personal gain.

Through the muck and mire
striving to a higher plane
my life not the same
but no growth
in casting blame.

Through dark crevices
of my profound experiences
keeping my head held high.

There are days
feeling like I can fly
others...
wandering toward demise
faith compels me
to give another try.

Still...
there are long painful nights
with no end in sight.

I still awake
paining over my plight
still I fight
till I see the light.

Thanks to the Master
I find strength to press
my life reminds me

of a game of chess
coming to a painful crest
attest I must.

Hearts are broken
my life's a token
testimony to life's
hurts and pains ill spoken
no time for joking.

Through my hurtful past
no doubt
a positive influence on society
teaching precepts of propriety.

Through my profound
hurts and pains
impressing...possessing in me
a better character
if only released
from my legal oppressor.

I'd gladly live in exile
constantly perfecting
my profile
never again live in denial.

To all the precious sistas
hurt by me
tried loving me
I'm preparing profound apologies
reverencing them
in all my anthologies.

Still...
as I prepare

Khanemuism

going through this
tremendous rain of pain.

Flooding my veins
my heart often hurts to exclaim
trying to explain my pain.

Deeply painful
carrying the mark of stigma
hoping you
can feel my dilemma.

I've absorbed
so many painful emotions
I'm more than ready
for a pleasant promotion.

Robert L. Woods 'Khanemu'

WHEN THINGS FALL APART

When life's storms arise
seeming to wash away
your most treasured dreams.

Causing you to wade
in a sea of despair
the blowback
of emotional pain
seems too much to bare.

Remember there is someone
who really loves you
cares for you.

Someone there to lift you
encourage you
someone there always
with open arms.

That someone is me
I will always love
support...
and adore you.

Chapter 7
The Sacredness Of Eulogies

The passing of loved ones becomes strong pillars, girded in our memory, entrenched in our emotions, affecting our joys, our sorrows, our longings--yet keeping us, balanced, firm, and upright. They become the mighty columns of our being.

__KHANEMU

Robert L. Woods 'Khanemu'

A STAR ROSE; THEN FADED COMPLETELY

A star rose bright
for all to see,
the brightest star
in my family's tree.
Her beauty shined immensely
she was my sister you see

She was a star
that gleamed
total fulfillment
of a parent's dream.

A woman who loved in
gentleness and slender
heart of gold,
never a pretender.

She shined bright,
then faded fast.
On that dreadful night
was my sister's last.

Her passing brought
brawling billows of
heart-ache and pain
perpetual tears became
our pillow's stain.
Family and friends came
mourning in the rain.

Family and friends
loved when she was around.
mention of her name
commenced the sweetest sound.

Khanemuism

Heart-broken because
we lost her too soon.
She was a flower in full bloom
Didn't know danger loomed,
she now rests in a tomb.

Can't believe a sister
so beautiful
could pass from the scene,
how could life be so mean.
She still lives in our dreams.

She was my sister you see
ravishing sister with
the sweetest personality.

Oh please tell me
why sweet Cindy
had to leave us.
Our tears seeped
through the earth's crust.
Cindy has returned to the dust.

She possessed the brightest
of possibilities,
then swallowed by tragedy's misery
propelled into eternity's mystery.
She will be an everlasting memory

She was my sister you see,
the brightest star
in my family's tree.

in loving memory of-Cynthia Chloe Jackson

Robert L. Woods 'Khanemu'

DAD IS FREE

Hard to believe,
Dad is gone,
our dad's work is done.

The master,
has called you home,
to live everlasting,
around his throne.

From dawn,
to dust,
a father we could trust.

Always a man,
with something to do,
now you're gone,
and we've lost the glue.

Dad was an example,
of what a father,
should be,
caring, loving, responsible,
to his family and community.

You've been a good father,
husband with a heart of gold,
one of the last,
of a marvelous fold,
perpetual memory,
to be told.

We take this day to mourn,
with tears and flowers,

remembering the love,
Daddy showered.

So love with kisses,
and hugs,
never with hisses and shrugs,
before God pulls the plug.

You lived a good life,
for all to see,
we're honored,
to be part,
of your family's tree,
Rejoicing to know,
Dad is finally free.

our beloved Dad...is definitely free.

Robert L. Woods 'Khanemu'

MOM'S DANCE WITH ETERNITY

Beloved mother, your time has come,
88 long years,
Now your consummation,
Spiritual consecration.

Sorrow, sickness, and death,
Lost their dominion,
Cast ---- like,
A burden garment.

Go be free, free as your spirit can be,
Take your seat,
Amongst angelic voices.

Sing magnificent hymns,
With prophets of old,
Fellowship with GOD's martyrs,
Righteous over- comers.

When you reach eternity,
Say hello to Uncle Roy,
Papa Cruz and Cindy for me.

Dear Mother,
We won't stay sad,
We'll miss you, love you,
Never forget you.

We heard,
Your daughter's testimony,
A mother well – loved,
Well cared for.

Khanemuism

Your son- in law, comforted you,
Your daughter paid homage to you,
Stuck by you,
Since your fountain of youth.

You spoke words,
Of gratitude,
Of praise and thanks.

Bearing witness,
Of your weary life's journey.

GOD's messenger,
Perched by your side,
Whispering in your ear.

God on His throne,
Ready for your soul's bounty.

The last hour, your weary head,
Pressed on your pillow,
Soon afterwards,
A deep silence.

Surrendered your breath,
Crossed over,
Then the Pass- over,
Blessed succession of events.

With loving hearts, farewell to you,
As your earthly remains mingle,
With your soul mate,
Fertilizing,
The sod dense earth.

Your remains,
Withering among,
The elements,
We hear nature's symphony,
Rhythm ... of the four winds.

Access to GOD's
Jubilee granted,
No more,
Trials and fasting,
Joy everlasting.

Expressing,
The longitude,
And Latitude,
Of our gratitude ...
GOD speed to you.

Your Spirit, risen,
Bright mysterious,
As the ether,
Three days shy of Easter.

Enlivened,
Emboldened,
Never to be conquered again.

We hear you,
Laughing at death,
What is death?
A change in destination,
A transfiguration.

Flesh to Spirit,
Earth to heaven,

Khanemuism

Life, death,
Then life eternal

Dear Mother,
GOD gave you life's mystery,
You're more,
Then a passing memory,
You are our future,
And history.

88 long years,
Now your consummation,
Spiritual consecration,
We're solemnly gathered,
For your vindication

With all our blessings,
Enjoy your dance with eternity.

MOM'S MOST BLESSED MOMENT

Dear Mother,

Your most blessed moment is here,
a cross roads ushering you into another sphere,
a heavenly realm where saints and seers abide.

No more traveling, treading through this cold, cold earth,
filled with uncertainties, troubles,
sickness and disease.

Dear Momma-you are truly free,
free to create, to laugh and rejoice as you breathe
your eternal sigh of relief,
life can be brief, you lived it the best you could be.

The Master with his outstretched hands-
guiding you to your blessed resting place,
for your soul to receive, all your worries,
worldly concerns have been put to ease,
your loving memory never ceasing to be.

Your legacy is filled with love for your sons,
love for your daughters, tremendous love for your family,
overflowing love for your grandkids,
no one loved as precious, as kind as you did.

We come mourning you, some with heavy hearts and tears,
salted with sorrows,
the memory of you will always brighten our coming years,
and tomorrows.

You were never a token Mother,
rather, a Mother like no other,
so we honor you with our tears,
hearts and minds.

Khanemuism

You were the glue, the binding knot,
keeping us all together,
now your eternal wish...for us to become much better,
better brothers, better sisters, much closer to family.

As your body withers, refreshing and fertilizing
God's nutrient rich earth, your love and laughter,
your caring spirit lives with each of us,
as a piercing light, illuminating our path as we
motion through this conflicted world.

We can proudly say you were a good Mother,
with a heart of gold,
one of the last of a marvelous fold.

Robert L. Woods 'Khanemu'

Dear Mother,

Your blessed moment is here,
an emotional atmosphere filled with love and tears,
a cross road...ushering you into your heavenly sphere,
your loving memory - we will always hold preciously dear.

If there is a reader that would like more information or
may have any questions and would like to reach out to the author,
please contact him at:

Robert L. Woods #AC8749
CTF Central – C Wing - #316L
P.O. Box 689
Soledad, CA 93960

About the Author

After embarking on a transformative creative writing journey nine years ago, Robert L. Woods has evolved to a level of looking at every aspect of the world through a poetic lens with the aim of delving below the surface, revealing its many meanings and significance in relation to our human predicament.

He is a passionately powerful spoken-word poet in addition to being an articulate and captivating speaker in Toastmasters International, using his impressive baritone voice to add to his stage presence.

He has performed introductions for a couple of rap groups in the Bay Area and most notably is the introduction voice on a video honoring the late Dr. Leon Goldman, father of Senator Dianne Feinstein, at the Moscone Center in 2008.

Woods is sensitive to the complex racial/ethnic struggles and conflicts, as well as geopolitical and corporate injustice affecting the economic plight of the masses in the United States and abroad. He meticulously and poetically uses his pen to illuminate these sensitive subjects for his readers in satire, poem, and prose.

Printed in the United States
By Bookmasters